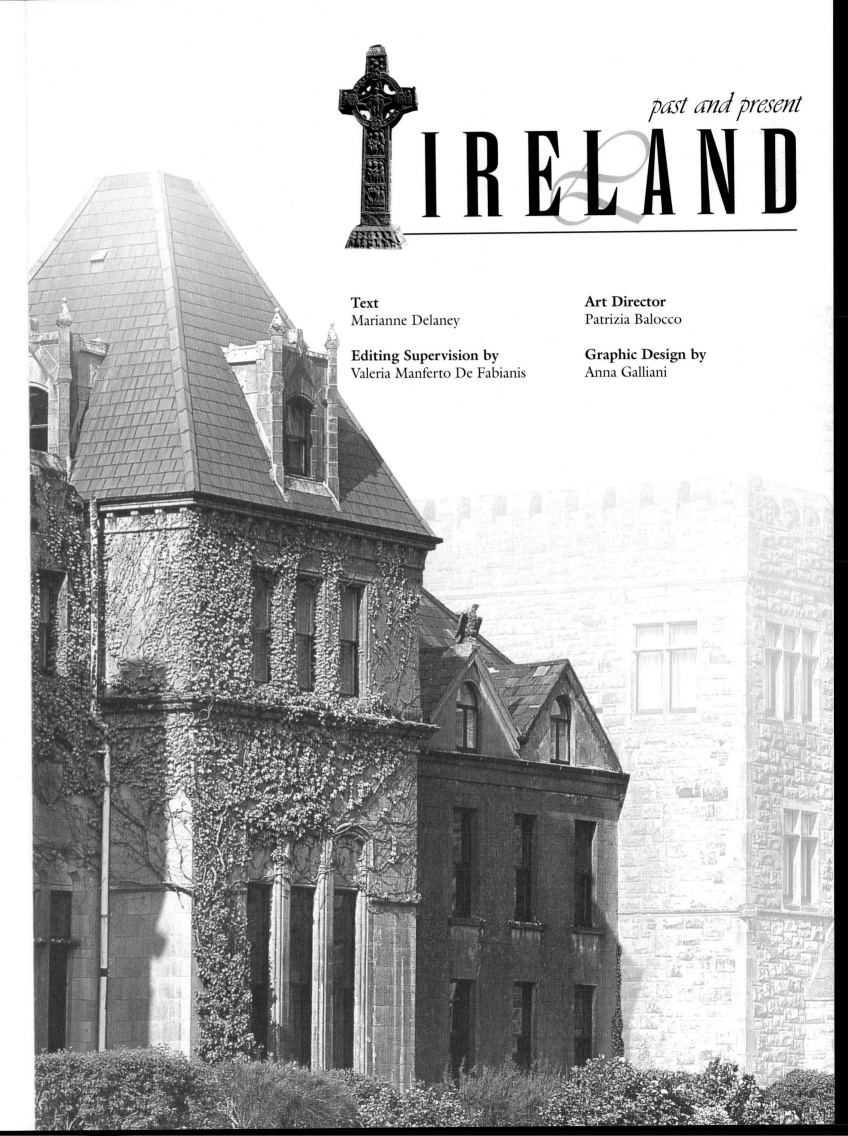

past and present

IRELAND

Text
Marianne Delaney

Art Director
Patrizia Balocco

Editing Supervision by
Valeria Manferto De Fabianis

Graphic Design by
Anna Galliani

TIGER BOOKS INTERNATIONAL

CONTENTS

1 Fanad Head, at the tip of the lovely Fanad peninsula in county Donegal, offers one of the most spectacular views of the northwest coasts of Ireland.

2 and 7 Ashford Castle in Cong, County Mayo is a 19th-century neo-Gothic expansion of an 18th-century French-style chateau, which, in turn, was constructed from the remnants of a 13th-century Norman Castle.

3, 4, 5 and 6 The Dingle Peninsula in County Kerry is a romantic paradise of cliffs, beaches, mountains, hills of flowering heather, and rich green fields enclosed by low drystone walls. Dingle's Atlantic coastline is rough, wild, and remote; it is an Irish-speaking stronghold (Gaeltacht) and home to many prehistoric and Early Christian sites.

8-9 Green and blue, the most prevalent colours of the Irish countryside. Green by definition, Ireland's gentle hills and meadows dominate the island. The over 800 lakes (loughs) that are scattered throughout the land were created by the gradual receding of glaciers that covered the surface of the island approximately 10,000 years ago. But legends provide more enchanting explanations, such as the infinite tears of star-crossed lovers.

© 1996 White Star S.r.l.
Via Sassone, 22/24
13100 Vercelli, Italy

This edition published in 1997 by TIGER BOOKS INTERNATIONAL PLC, 26a York Street Twickenham TW1 3LJ, England.

ISBN 1-85501-913-2

Printed in Italy by Grafedit, Bergamo (Italy).
Colour separations by Scanner Service, Verona (Italy).

INTRODUCTION

Ireland is a country which is uniquely associated with a single colour—green. The visitor to Ireland is immediately struck by the myriad of greens in this soft and gentle land of hills and small valleys, but then one becomes aware of the blues: sky blue, a surprising azure in a place where the weather changes by the moment; lake blue, the deep sapphire of hundreds of little loughs scattered across the land; and sea blue, a vibrant metallic colour, sometimes calm, sometimes disquieting.

Against the green and blue, there lies always the colour of stone, the stone of the raw, magnificent cliff or the massive landscape of barren rock. The stone of towns and cities opens up to a countryside littered with stone remains, each revealing something of the island's past. A maze of stone walls tells of centuries of farming poor and unrewarding land, monastic ruins speak of the simple solitude of saints and scholars, and towers and castles tell tales of invaders and marauders. Much is divulged by stone—great houses proclaim the opulence of the once powerful, while cottage ruins testify to the sufferings of the once oppressed.

When the weather takes a turn, sea and sky also pale to stone: greys dominate, accented only by neutral patches of livestock and roadsigns. But then, suddenly, bursts of red, yellow, violet or pink materialize; the eye is startled, not only by blooming hedgerows of gorse or fuscia, but also by the faces of tiny houses, shopfronts—anywhere and everywhere. Walls, doors and windowframes become places where the imagination runs wild, where bright colours are used to ward off damp weather, damp spirits—to play pranks on the intruder.

It is this playful spirit which reflects an essential element of the Irish temperament—to face difficulty with wit, to encounter defeat with a sense of humour. Misfortune is met with reassurance: "it could be worse." And in a land that has had its share of tragedies, this is certainly true. Here, hospitality is revered; the lack of it not forgotten. And in rural communities throughout Ireland, neighbour will not see neighbour "stuck," be it for the essentials of life, help saving hay or simply "a bit of company."

Any time is a good time for a chat, whether in the middle of town, on the side of the road, in a shop, at a bus stop or fireside. Gathering in the pub or coffeeshop is a way of life, born of the desire for good company,

good conversation and often a bit of good music. To drop in on neighbours, hear the news, share a story and a bit of a laugh is a national priority. Conversation is an art, filled with offbeat nuance, elegant phrasing and wild metaphor.

The dual linguistic tradition of Irish Gaelic and English enhances the grace of the spoken and written word so that this small country has made an unparalleled contribution to world literature, while maintaining a distinctive oral tradition of storytelling and a complex structure of language and usage in everyday speech. Whether the result of poverty, isolation, rebellious nationalism, or conscious revivals, folk tradition in Ireland remains strong, and is manifest in the music, verse, dance, crafts, festivals, customs and remnants of superstitious belief that still pervade the society.

In a land where legend and history overlap, where the collective popular imagination embraces a legacy of fairies, bards, heroes and giants, where the persecution of the population remained a constant for hundreds of years, and where the beauty of the landscape is often deeply moving, the inspiration for writers abounds. In 1995, poet Seamus Heaney joined that roster of Irish Nobel laureates that includes Shaw, Yeats and Beckett. Modern writers as diverse as Brian Friel, Maeve Binchy and Roddy Doyle have become internationally famous for the visions of Ireland that they have brought to audiences throughout the world.

Naturally, it would be a mistake to place Ireland in some unreal dimension between a fairy tale and an old watercolour. On the contrary, this is a lively and vital country, whose people are confronted daily by the realities of the violent conflict in Northern Ireland, religious scandals involving clergy, and social controversies such as the legalization of divorce, only achieved in the Republic by a narrow margin in 1995. This

10 top Natural repossession. Over time, vegetation may overwhelm stone walls, making the two indistinguishable.

10-11 Ireland is a country of small towns and villages, consisting of clusters of houses around a church, post office, pub and shops.

11 right A traditional thatched cottage. The three-room stone houses that once dominated rural Ireland have been almost completely replaced by modern, bungalow-style homes.

"new" Ireland manages to coexist in harmony with the old, creating an exciting synergy between the traditional and the modern.

This energy is most easily observed in Dublin, where traditional music often yields to rock, and scores of musicians pursue fame in the footsteps of such international stars as U2, Sinead O'Connor and The Cranberries, while traditional groups such as the Chieftains collaborate on recordings with Mick Jagger, Marianne Faithful and Van Morrison. Meanwhile, rock festivals are held on castle grounds, arts centres open in abandoned prisons, and health-food shops thrive under ancient archways.

And if literature and music clearly lead the way, an explosion in the visual arts and an exciting young film industry demonstrate a new-found confidence in the arts not traditionally associated with Ireland. The films of Jim Sheridan, including *My Left Foot* and *In the Name of the Father*, have won numerous Academy Awards and brought uniquely Irish stories to world attention.

But always beyond the cities there silently beckons a background of exquisite beauty, dubbed by William Butler Yeats "the land of heart's desire." Capable at once of offering both the absolute freedom of wide open spaces and the sense of being under a spell, this magical place captivates the visitor with its enchanting world of castles, fortresses, ancient abbeys and prehistoric dolmens. The "heart's desire" will surely be fulfilled for those who are willing to abandon itineraries, suspend time and surrender their imagination to Ireland's complex terrain of rugged landscapes and verdant countryside, its old cities and tiny villages, and its people, language and traditions.

12-13 Muckross
House, a lovely
Tudor-style residence
built in 1843 on the
shores of Muckross
Lough in the heart of

Killarney National
Park, today houses the
headquarters of the
Kerry Folklife
Centre.

Dunluce Castle in Ulster

Tory Island

Rathlin Island

Aran Island

Gweebarra Bay

Londonderry
(Derry)

Bann

Belfast

Bangor

Donegal

Foyle

Lough Neagh

Lagan

Donegal Bay

Sligo

Lower
Lough
Erne

Upper Lough
Erne

Ulster Canal

Newry Canal

Inishkea

Lough
Gill

Lough
Allen

Mourne
Mountains

Lough
Conn

Dundalk Bay

Westport

Castlebar

Longford

Boyne

Lough
Mask

Lough
Ree

Royal Canal

Irish
Sea

Clifden

Lough
Corrib

Athlone

Dublin

Galway

Galway Bay

Grand Canal

Aran Islands

Bray

St. George's Channel

Atlantic
Ocean

Lough
Derg

Nore

Wicklow
Mountains

Shannon

Limerick

Kilkenny

Slaney

Feale

Barrow

Tralee

Suir

Wexford

Dingle Bay

Killarney

Blackwater

Waterford

Lough
Leane

Laune

Cork

Bantry

Kinsale

Bantry Bay

The countryside in County Cork

A beach in County Donegal

Donegall Square in Belfast

The pastures of County Waterford

A view of Dublin from the River Liffey

21 top left The
Poulnabrone Dolmen
is located in the
"Burren" in County
Clare, an area rich in
prehistoric sites.
Dolmens are the
remains of Stone Age
portal graves, formed
of three or more
upright stones covered
by a large horizontal
capstone, and once
enclosed in an earth
mound. Dolmen is a
Breton word meaning
"stone table."

20-21 *The passage
grave at Newgrange,
County Meath is one of
the most impressive and
best preserved
prehistoric burial sites
in all of Europe.
Dating back to about
3,000 B.C., the
enormous mound
enclosing the tomb—
280 feet in diameter
and 40 feet high—was
originally surrounded
by engraved menhirs
(upright boulders), a
dozen of which survive.
Horizontal kerbstones
which encircle the
mound are carved with
concentric, spiral, and
zigzag designs. The
long passageway is
similarly decorated,
and leads to a main
underground chamber
and three smaller side
chambers, each of which
contains a ritual basin
(photo lower left). An
opening above the
entrance is designed to
allow the sun to shine
directly down the 66-
foot passageway into the
main chamber at
dawn on the day of the
winter solstice.*

T he first archaeological traces of human activity in Ireland date from about 7,000 B.C. These Mesolithic (Middle Stone Age) people lived by fishing, hunting and food gathering, until their Late Stone Age followers cleared large tracts of land and introduced farming around 3,500 B.C. It was these Neolithic peoples who constructed the first megalithic tombs—dolmens, passage graves and court cairns—that are found throughout Ireland. One of the most magnificent examples of these in Europe can be seen at Newgrange in County Meath. An enormous mound covers this 4,500-year-old burial site, and many intricate spiral and zigzag carvings are found on its stones.

The many stone circles and standing stones throughout the country date from Bronze Age (2000–500 B.C.) migrations that brought metalworking skills to the production of tools, weapons and ornaments. It was during the Iron Age of superior weaponry (500 B.C.–400A.D.) that the Celts, and later, Christianity and literacy, came to Ireland.

It is presumed that the Celts, who had also settled throughout most of Europe, did not arrive in Ireland in very large numbers, but were instead a rather powerful minority. Though pre-Celtic customs and many traces of older, non-Celtic tongues survive in the Irish language, these predecessor populations were eventually dominated and Celticized by the middle of the first millennium A.D.

The history of the Irish really begins here, when the populations on the island melded and came to share a common language and culture. The Celtic influence on Irish civilization was more enduring than in other areas of their European infiltration, partly because of the island's remote

21 top right The
stone circle at
Ardgroom, County
Cork. Stone circles or
henges are circular
arrangements of
upright, free-
standing stones, most
dating from the
Bronze Age. These
isolated groups of
menhirs are
associated with
burials, rituals, and
assemblies, and may
have been used for
measuring the sun's
shadow for the
determination of a
seasonal calendar.
Hundreds of stone
circles are found
throughout Ireland
today.

geography, but also because neither Roman occupation nor the barbarian raids which followed the empire's fall ever reached Ireland.

In Ireland, the Celtic Gaels lived in an agricultural society based upon kinship units known as *fine*, or joint families. These extended for several generations of male kin from which a *derbfhine*, or leader, was selected. A system of kings (*rí*) ruled the land, with many lower kings reigning over tribes, or *tuatha*. They, in turn, were

ruled by over-kings (*ruiri*), who later were subject to the kings of over-kings (*rí ruirech*) who ruled the province and held their seats at Tara in County Meath and Cashel in County Tipperary. Out of over 150 petty dominions, five emerged as the leading Gaelic kingdoms, roughly corresponding to the four present-day provinces of Ireland: Ulster in the north, Leinster in the east, Connaught in the west and Munster in the south. They also included the smaller Kingdom of Meath, which

22 top right The Ardagh Chalice was discovered accidentally in 1868 by a boy gathering potatoes near a ring fort in County Limerick. It is one of the most beautiful examples of early Irish Christian art, dating from the 8th century. Made of hammered silver, it is decorated with bronze, gold filigree and coloured glass studs.

22 left The Golden Boat was found in a field at Broighter, County Derry, and dates from approximately the first century A.D. The model is fitted with a mast, oars, and seats for rowers.

22 bottom right The finely worked silver fibula is probably from the Viking era; the Vikings supplied local artisans with most of their silver.

23 top left The splendid Tara Brooch dates from the 8th century, and is made from silver-gilt and gold foil. It is decorated with interlaced gold filigree, and amber and glass studs, which form a particularly elegant design of birds and wild animals, scrolls and spirals.

23 bottom left Medieval ornamental objects are one of the greatest legacies of the distant Irish past, when artisans created not only precious reliquaries and religious objects, but also fine jewellery. Gold ornaments of remarkable skill, created by Irish metalworkers as far back as the Bronze Age, have been discovered.

23 top right An aerial view of Dún Aenghus, an ancient promontory fort on Inishmore, the largest of the Aran Islands. The Iron-Age fort has a triple layer of semi-circular stone walls that end abruptly at the edge of a sheer cliff. Thousands of sharp upright boulders form an additional outer defence. Legend holds that it was built by a prehistoric race, the "Fir Bolg."

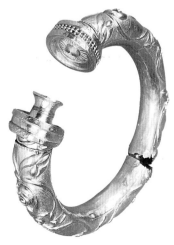

23 bottom right Torques, either neckrings or bracelets, such as this example from the Broighter hoard, date mainly from the Bronze Age.

eventually became assumed into Leinster.

In a society with no central government, towns or currency, battles between *tuatha* and wars between kingdoms were often waged over cattle. Tens of thousands of ring-forts (*raths*), hill forts, promontory forts and crannogs, or islet forts, were built during this period to protect kinship groups from each other's raids. The Celtic Gaels placed great emphasis on art and learning and held their *aes dána* (men of art) class of poets, druids, bards and historians in great esteem. Their highly codified system of Brehon Law was remarkable for its respect for the property and divorce rights of women.

The fact that Christianity had gained a foothold in Ireland by the middle of the fifth century A.D. is attributed to missionaries like Patrick, who, according to legend, converted the land single-handedly. This patron saint of Ireland first came to the island as a teenage slave, kidnapped during Irish raids on the Welsh coast. He fled after six years, became a monk and returned to Ireland to convert the country, which is said to have been accomplished in A.D. 432.

As the Celtic Gaels adopted the Christian faith, often an entire *tuath* would leave their *rath* to take up the ascetic life in monastic settlements. The monastic site at *Sceiligh Micheál* (Skellig Michael) in the Skellig Islands off the coast of Kerry is a remarkably intact example of these settlements. The stone beehive cells and tiny oratories that hug the cliff

24 top left and right Splendid illuminations adorn The Book of Kells (8th or early 9th century), the manuscript of the four gospels. Considered one of the most beautiful books in the world, it is on display in the Old Library at Trinity College. The Virgin and Child are depicted in the upper left photo, and, above right, a richly illuminated capital from the Gospel of St. Matthew.

24 centre An image of St. Patrick, Ireland's patron saint, wearing bishop's vestments. The background landscape represents the coast of Mayo, where the sacred mountain of Croagh Patrick stands. It was from this summit, according to legend, that Patrick drove the snakes—a Christian symbol of evil—out of Ireland.

24 bottom The Cross of Muiredach, dating from the 10th century, is one of the three great crosses at the abbey of Monasterboice in County Louth, and one of the finest of the Irish high crosses. Perfectly preserved for 1,000 years, the carved relief work depicts scenes from the Bible and the Crucifixion of Christ.

25 This richly illuminated page of The Book of Kells, with Jesus at the centre, is also part of the Gospel of St. Matthew.

26 left *The illustration shows Viking boats in the 9th century. The first Viking incursions against the monasteries of Britain and Ireland began in A.D. 795 with raids at Iona off the coast of Scotland, one of the settlements of the Irish missionary Columba. By A.D. 841, the Vikings had settled the Irish coast and founded the first cities of Dublin and Waterford.*

26 right *After taking over the reign of Munster in A.D. 976, and usurping the power of the Ui Neill dynasty, the Irish hero Brian Boru then challenged the Vikings and their Leinster allies, defeating them at the Battle of Clontarf in 1014. However, he himself was killed at the moment of victory, and the internecine wars for the high-kingship of Ireland continued.*

were built with such precision that they remain watertight to this day.

The monasteries grew in size and influence, and by the eighth century, while the rest of Europe declined into the Dark Ages, art and literacy flourished in these secluded communes of Irish Christianity. Richly carved high crosses, illuminated manuscripts and fine metalwork of holy vessels and ornamental adornments date from this period. The Ardagh Chalice and the Tara Brooch are outstanding examples of the intricate gold filigree work of the monastic artisans, and are on display at the National Museum in Dublin. The Book of Kells—the most splendid of the illuminated manuscripts—is an elaborately illustrated Latin transcription of the four gospels. Once stored in the monastery at Kells, it is now on view at Trinity College in Dublin.

Viking raids on Ireland and Britain began at the end of the eighth

27 top Richard FitzGilbert de Clare, the Earl of Pembroke and better known as Strongbow is pictured here with his brother. Strongbow led the Anglo-Norman invasion of Ireland in 1169, setting the stage for the English government in Ireland.

27 bottom A woodcut from John Derrick's derogatory "Image of Irelande." A noble chieftain and his entourage dine in an outdoor feast, while a pair of men warm their posteriors by the fire. Amid the gathering, a friar preaches and a bard and his harper entertain. The bards were later persecuted by the English, when some forms of Irish culture were banned.

28 A 1616 map of
the realm of Ireland.
The representative
figures of the social
classes include, at the
top, "The
Gentleman" and
"The Gentlewoman,"
and on the bottom,
"The Wild Irish
Man," and "The
Wild Irish Woman."

century and devastated many of the monastic settlements, including Iona, which had been founded by the Irish saint Columba in A.D. 563. The surviving monks fled and relocated to Kells in County Meath. Round towers, built at monastic sites after the start of these onslaughts, served as belfries, lookout posts and shelters from attack. Over eighty of the towers still stand in Ireland today, and are slender structures, tapering to heights of between sixty and one hundred feet.

Though they left a trail of brutality and destruction, the Vikings also established the first cities in Ireland, including Dublin, Waterford and Limerick, and taught the Irish navigation and shipbuilding. Dynastic

wars among the Irish kings continued for centuries. By A.D. 1002, "Brian Boru" (*Brian Bóroimhe*) of Munster had besieged all the kingdoms of the land and declared himself high-king (*ard-rí*) of Ireland. But at the famous Battle of Clontarf in A.D. 1014, when Brian Boru's decisive defeat of the Vikings should have sealed his absolute power, he was killed.

As this ever-shifting balance of power played itself out, the Anglo-Normans invaded Ireland in A.D. 1169, led by Richard FitzGilbert de Clare, Earl of Pembroke and better known as Strongbow. Leinster fell under their control within two years. The monarch, Henry II, armed with the authority of the Pope, proceeded to grant fiefs in Ireland to Norman nobles until they held an extensive tract of land in the east that became known as the Pale.

In response to the lax discipline and abuses of power in Irish monasteries, a stricter, diocesan system of Christianity was introduced during the twelfth century and abbeys for the new religious orders of Cistercians, Augustinians, Dominicans and Franciscans were erected soon after. Norman confiscations spread throughout Ireland, and by the middle of the thirteenth century, they occupied over two-thirds of the island. Henry II ruled the colony through King's Councils, which eventually evolved into an Irish parliament.

As the Anglo-Normans settled in Ireland, their assimilation with the indigenous people alarmed the king's representatives to such an extent that they enacted the Statutes of Kilkenny in 1366. These first of many anti-Irish penal codes to follow forbade intermarriage and the use of the Irish language, customs and dress.

THE
KINGDOME
OF IRLAND
Devided into severall Provinces, and the
againe devided into Counties.
Newly described.

28-29 This 19th-
century painting by
Charles Louis Muller,
part of the collection
of the Museum of
Fine Arts in Lyons,
France, depicts Oliver

Cromwell's banishment of Irish Catholics in 1655. Cromwell confiscated two-thirds of the territory held by Irish landowners,

murdered hundreds of thousands of Irish natives and sent their orphaned children to work as slaves in the British West Indies.

29 top left Portrait of Henry VIII (1492–1547) painted by Hans Holbein in 1540. During his reign, Henry VIII had himself declared "supreme head on earth" of the Churches of England and Ireland, and "king of Ireland." His Protestant Reformation marked the beginning of centuries of great repression of Irish Catholicism and brutal colonial policy towards the island.

29 top right The repressive policy towards Ireland intensified under Oliver Cromwell (1599–1658), shown here in a portrait by Lely Pieter. The ruthless massacres perpetuated by the anti-royalist and his parliamentary army of "Ironsides," who razed towns and cities to the ground, are infamous.

Nevertheless, the integration continued, prompting the passage of Poynings Law which subordinated the Irish Parliament to complete control by the Parliament in London in 1494.

By the sixteenth century, the Anglo-Norman aristocracy had become "more Irish than the Irish themselves," profoundly changing Ireland. Markets, towns and cities grew up around their Gothic-style castles and cathedrals, while their fortified tower-house residences became a common feature of the Irish landscape.

In 1536, Henry VIII broke with the Pope in Rome and declared himself "supreme head on earth" of the Churches of England and Ireland.

The Reformation brought a systematic repression of Catholicism that began with the dissolution of the monasteries. By 1541, Henry VIII had assumed the title of King of Ireland, and the Tudor land policies of "surrender and regrant" and "plantation," began dispossessing the Irish in favour of loyal English settlers.

Resistance to the colonization and religious repression during the Elizabethan period gave rise to serious uprisings by Irish earldoms which were supported by the Pope and Catholic Spain. The Desmond rebellions in Munster were quashed in 1580, while the Nine Years War of Ulster chiefs Hugh O'Neill and Red Hugh O'Donnell ended with their

defeat alongside the Spanish at the Battle of Kinsale in 1601. Their eventual exile, known as "The Flight of the Earls," left Ulster open to English and Scottish settlers.

A peasant rising against the Protestant planters in Ulster which led to the slaughter of thousands of people, brought Oliver Cromwell to Irish shores in 1649. After repressing the rebellion, he launched his infamous campaign of genocide and destruction throughout the country, sending the Catholic Irish to "Hell or Connaught"—the infertile lands of the west. At the completion of his conquest, over three-quarters of Irish land had been expropriated. At the Battle of the Boyne in 1690, the dispossessed Catholic monarch of England, James II, was defeated by the Protestant King William of Orange, a victory which still galvanizes Northern Ireland loyalists today.

The eighteenth century was marked by complete political, cultural and religious oppression of the native Irish, as manifest in the penal laws that forbade then the right to own land, vote, hold public office, maintain schools, practise their faith, speak the Irish language or play Irish music. Catholics, Presbyterians, Baptists, Methodists and Quakers were all affected by the laws until 1828. Near the end of the century, the sentiments of the American and French Revolutions inspired the Irish. Enlightened Protestants like Wolfe Tone organized the United Irishmen to

Parliament, and the passage of the Catholic Emancipation Act of 1829. His pacifist, constitutional approach to Irish freedom alienated hard-line nationalists, and he finally withdrew from politics in 1846.

34 top Tensions in the mid-19th century multiplied. In 1848, a revolt organized by the Young Irelanders was repressed by the English, a pattern which repeated itself regularly during the Land War agitations of the early 1880s.

34-35 The Land League organized a riot in Limerick in October, 1881. As well as the goals of land reform and abolishing evictions, those in support of the Irish cause recognized the need for self-government or Home Rule. This became the driving force of the Irish Parliamentary Party.

35 top Charles Stewart Parnell, chairman of the Irish Parliamentary Party since 1880, leading a party assembly in 1886.

35 centre Not everyone was in favour of Home Rule. The Unionist Party of Ulster Protestants took a firm stand in opposition to Parnell's party, and riots against Home Rule broke out.

35 bottom Emigration continued to be the choice of many as fear and tension continued to mount. Ships loaded with Irish emigrants left ports such as Liverpool in England, most headed for America. By the early 1900s, the island's pre-Famine population of eight million was reduced by half.

36 top An image of early 19th-century Dublin shows the General Post Office on Sackville Street (now O'Connell Street), and the enormous pillar honouring Britain's Admiral Nelson. The pillar was blown up in 1966 on the 50th anniversary of the Easter Rising.

36-37 A coloured engraving of the Rock of Cashel showing the ruins of St. Patrick's Cathedral, Cormac's Chapel and the Archbishop's Palace.

37 top right The
Rotunda Rooms,
where concerts were
held to finance the
attached hospital,
were designed by
Richard Cassels
(Castle) in the mid-
18th century, and
now house a cinema.

Dr. Bartholomew
Mosse established the
Rotunda, the first
public maternity
hospital in Europe.
The image shows
Parnell Square as it
appeared in the late
1700s (then Rutland
Square).

37 bottom right A
painting by T.S.
Roberts of Dublin
Castle as it appeared
in 1800, prior to the
remodelling and
reconstruction which
took place later in the
century.

fight discrimination against Catholics. Their attempted rising in 1798, assisted by the French who joined them at Killala Bay, was defeated, and Wolfe Tone was sentenced to death.

By 1801, the Irish Parliament had been dissolved, and the Act of Union established a United Kingdom of Great Britain and Ireland. Two decades later, the election of Daniel O'Connell, a middle-class Catholic agitator, forced the admission of Catholics to Parliament that resulted in the passage of the Catholic Emancipation Act of 1829 which repealed the penal laws. But by 1845 a blight that destroyed the potato

crop—the staple of the native Irish diet—resulted in the Great Famine. Mass evictions left men, women and children starving to death in the open fields, while cargoloads of grain and livestock were shipped daily to England for profitable trade. Conservative estimates put the deathtoll of the famine at one million, while another one and a half million people were forced to emigrate. By the turn of the century, the population of Ireland had halved from eight million to four million people.

Despite this immense human tragedy, political initiatives did not cease. With the goal of an independent Ireland, the Fenian Brotherhood and the Irish Republican Brotherhood (IRB) were founded in 1858, while the Home Rule League in support of

39 top left An open letter from the journalist Francis Sheehy-Skeffington to a leader of the 1916 Rising, Thomas MacDonagh, expressing support for the cause. Despite the fact that he was a pacifist, Sheehy-Skeffington was arrested during the rising and shot by the British Army.

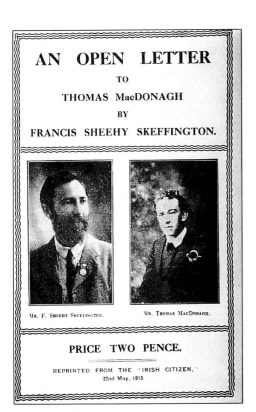

39 bottom left The 1916 Proclamation declaring an independent Irish Republic was read by Patrick Pearse from the steps of the General Post Office on Easter Monday. All seven of the signatories to the Proclamation were executed by firing squad, along with eight other leaders of the Rising.

39 top right British soldiers stand behind a makeshift barricade on Talbot Street in Dublin during the Easter Rising.

39 bottom right A view of the devastation of Dublin's city centre near O'Connell Bridge, following the 1916 Rising.

40 top Eamon de Valera (1882–1975) led a contingent of Irish Volunteers during the 1916 Rising, but was spared execution because of his American citizenship. His life was dedicated to the struggle for an independent, 32-county Irish Republic. He served as Taoiseach (Prime Minister) of Ireland from 1932 to 1948, and for two later periods of office.

40 bottom Arthur Griffith established the Sinn Féin ("We Ourselves") Party in 1905 to oppose British rule in Ireland. In the general election of 1918, De Valera led Sinn Féin to a sweeping victory in Ireland, which provided a mandate for severing ties with Britain and full Irish independence.

Irish autonomy was established in 1870. Its leader, Charles Parnell, was forced to retire on the eve of success due to a scandal involving adultery.

The early 1900s were marked by the founding of numerous organizations in support of Irish independence; Arthur Griffith's *Sinn Féin* ("We Ourselves") party was founded in 1905 and advocated resistance to British rule, while in 1913 nationalists organized the Irish Volunteers and the labour movement known as the Irish Citizens' Army. The next year, a Home Rule bill for Ireland was approved, but its enactment was suspended with the outbreak of the World War I.

Taking advantage of British preoccupations in France, a group of Irish Volunteers led by Patrick Pearse, along with a small contingent of the Irish Citizen Army led by James Connolly, marched into Dublin and occupied several strategic buildings. On Easter Monday in 1916, they proclaimed an independent Irish Republic from the steps of the General Post Office. The rising was over within a week, but the execution of its fifteen leaders stirred fierce nationalist sentiments.

In 1917, the Sinn Féin Party led by Eamon de Valera won the elections, but refused to take their seats in the London Parliament, instead establishing the *Dáil Éireann* (Irish Parliament) with its own Irish Republican Army (IRA). Britain responded by sending a vicious auxiliary force known as the Black and Tans, who terrorized the countryside in a murderous campaign to stamp out Irish nationalism. A truce was called in 1921 with the fateful signing of the Anglo-Irish Treaty, which approved of a twenty-six-county Irish Free State, leaving six northern counties within the United Kingdom.

41 *After the election, Sinn Féin representatives refused to sit in the British Parliament, instead establishing an independent Dáil Éireann (Irish Parliament) that assembled in Dublin from 1919 to 1921 (photo top left and bottom right). On December 6, 1921, the treaty establishing the Irish Free State was signed in London by an Irish delegation (centre) including Arthur Griffith (far left) and Michael Collins (seated centre). The treaty, narrowly ratified by the Dáil, left six Ulster counties as part of Great Britain and only granted Ireland dominion status in allegiance to the British Crown. De Valera and his supporters resigned in disgust and the nation split into civil war between Free State and anti-Treaty factions.*

The Dáil ratified the treaty by a narrow margin, but de Valera resigned in disgust and the nation split into civil war between free state and anti-treaty factions.

Following a cease-fire in 1923, two political parties emerged: the pro-treaty Fine Gael and the anti-treaty Fianna Fáil Parties. In 1932 de Valera and Fianna Fáil took office. Within five years, they approved an Irish Constitution, claiming on paper *Éire* (Ireland) as an independent, thirty-two-county state. In 1949, the twenty-six-county Republic of Ireland became completely independent of Britain, while the six partitioned counties in the North remained a part of the United Kingdom of Great Britain and Northern Ireland.

Discrimination against Catholics in employment, housing, education, public services and the electoral process in Northern Ireland gave rise to a grass-roots civil rights movement in the 1960s. When factional violence threatened to worsen, British troops were sent to the province in 1969 to restore peace and protect Catholics. Internment—the power to detain suspected activists without charge—was introduced. On what became known as Bloody Sunday in 1972, the British army opened fire on a civil rights march in Derry, killing thirteen unarmed Catholic demonstrators. Paramilitary groups like the nationalist IRA and the loyalist Ulster Defence Association (UDA) took up

arms, and the terrorist violence persisted into the next decade.

A famous hunger strike by IRA prisoners in 1981, demanding political rather than criminal status, left Bobby Sands and nine others dead. Support for the nationalist cause reached a peak in Ireland and throughout the world. But over the next fifteen years, IRA bombing campaigns soured many sympathizers, as scores of civilians, including children, were injured and killed. The violence on both sides, as well as abuses of power by the British Army, wearied the populace.

An IRA cease-fire was declared in August of 1994, followed by a significant reduction of British troops in the six counties. Eighteen months of calm set high hopes for All-Party Northern Ireland peacetalks scheduled for June of 1996, but IRA impatience with the British demands for preconditions to negotiation brought the cease-fire to an end when the paramilitaries

resumed their bombing campaign in February of 1996.

Limited peacetalks have begun with Sinn Féin—the political wing of the IRA led by Gerry Adams—absent from the table. Peace requires that a resolution be found between unionists who view themselves as a legal majority in support of the Union with Great Britain and nationalists who see that Union as an artificial remnant of eight hundred years of foreign occupation. Hopes that the polarized communities may reach some compromise in the near future are fragile, yet persistant.

42 The six counties partitioned by the 1921 Treaty were carved out of Ulster's nine counties and created a state with a Protestant majority; the region eventually became assumed into the United Kingdom of Great Britain and Northern Ireland. Decades of discrimination against Catholics in jobs, housing and public services, led to the civil rights movement of the 1960s. When Catholic protests met with loyalist and police violence, British troops were sent in. The paramilitary groups of the polarized communities took up arms and guerilla warfare ensued. Common scenes in 1970s Belfast included street riots (top right), soldiers and barbed wire barricades (centre) and civil rights marchers clashing with the British army (bottom left).

43 A large mural in Derry's Catholic Bogside district is dominated by a gruesome image of a boy in a gas mask wielding a homemade petrol bomb, one of the street weapons used by civilians, mainly youths, in sectarian rioting.

WE WANT PEACE

44 top left
"We want peace,"
says the banner held
by women during
a widely attended
march.

44 top right
Another large
demonstration cheers
the election of Gerry
Adams to the ranks
of Sinn Féin.

44-45 This photo,
shot on the day the
IRA announced
its cease-fire, shows
a child playing
happily. This symbolic
picture was published
in all the English
newspapers.

45 top The official
visit of American
President Bill

Clinton and his
wife Hillary was
a great event for
Ireland.

45 centre The leaders
of the two opposing
parties, John Hume
(left) and David
Trimble (right),
have spelled a
turning point
in Irish politics.

45 bottom Mary
Robinson, shown here
during festivities
celebrating her 1990
election as President
of Ireland, has also
played an active part

in the peace process.
She is also the first
Irish President
to have met the
Queen of England
during an official
visit.

THE ISLAND OF WRITERS

*T*hough the ancient culture, old ways, and indigenous language of the Irish people were nearly wiped out by the English policy of anglicization under the penal laws, only to be further decimated by famine and mass emigration, a vital Irish culture has survived, in most part thanks to its writers.

From the epic poetry and sagas of the ancient Gaelic Celts, to the Tony Award-winning dramas of Brian Friel, this "island of writers" has produced a body of fiction and verse that provides the world with a window to an extraordinary and unique culture. The dual linguistic heritage of Irish and English have provided the Irish writers of prose, poetry and drama with a fluency that has translated itself into a distinct national voice. The vast body of Irish literature, in Irish and English, has taken its place at the forefront of Western literature for centuries.

Anglo-Irish ascendancy dominated the early contribution to modern literature, beginning with the keen-witted Jonathan Swift. Born in Dublin in 1667, he served as dean of St. Patrick's Cathedral until his death in 1745. A socially-conscious intellectual, many of his satirical works, such as *A Modest Proposal for Preventing the Children of Ireland From Being A Burden* ... are a ferocious indictment of the economic oppression which the

46 Two of Ireland's Nobel laureates: Above right, William Butler Yeats (1865–1939) won the prestigious award in 1923, while George Bernard Shaw (1856–1950), below left, was bestowed with the honour in 1925.

English inflicted on Ireland. In this pamphlet, his suggestion that poor children be sold as meat to provide "a most delicious, nourishing and wholesome food" teems with savage irony. Swift's *Gulliver's Travels* is also a thinly disguised political satire on the gross class disparities of his day.

The Irish-born dramatist, poet and novelist Oliver Goldsmith—author of *She Stoops To Conquer, The Vicar of Wakefield* and the Famine-inspired poem "The Deserted Village"—lived out his life in London, as did his eighteenth-century contemporary Richard Brinsley Sheridan, who is best known for his play *The School for Scandal*. Both writers saw hugely successful productions of their comedic plays, which are still being performed around the world today.

Oscar Wilde was born in Dublin in 1854, but lived a fastidious English lifestyle in complete rebellion to his background (his mother, under the pen-name Speranza, contributed great outpourings of nationalistic verse to *The Nation*). Yeats summed up Wilde's career in Victorian London, stating that he "perpetually performed a play which was the opposite of all that he had known in childhood and youth." His glorious comedies, including *The Importance of Being Ernest*, are astute send-ups of upper-class English stereotypes. His *Ballad of Reading Gaol* is based on his prosecution and imprisonment for homosexual activity, after which he moved to Paris.

Wilde's contemporary, George Bernard Shaw, abandoned his Synge Street home in Dublin in 1876 (his restored house at No. 33 is open to visitors) to follow his mother to London where she had escaped her

47 James Joyce (1882–1941) and Samuel Beckett (1906–1989) both spent long periods of their lives in Paris. Joyce (above) lived in the French capital for 19 years, from 1920 to 1939, where he published Ulysses *and wrote* Finnegan's Wake. *Beckett (below) settled permanently in Paris in 1936, where he worked as Joyce's secretary for a time. He received the Nobel Prize for Literature in 1969.*

alcoholic husband. A dramatist and critic, he was dedicated to social reform. The cynical humour associated with his plays is evident in *Man and Superman, Major Barbara* and *Pygmalion* which was remade as the musical *My Fair Lady.* He was awarded the Nobel Prize for Literature in 1925.

The Irish Literary Revival, or Celtic Renaissance, of the late nineteenth century was led by William Butler Yeats (1865–1939). Born in Dublin and educated in England, he co-founded the Irish National Theatre at the Abbey. Fascinated by spiritualism and the occult, he delved into the mystical sagas and folktales of the Gaelic past in order to incorporate their heroes and stories into a new national literature of Ireland. He joined the Irish Republican Brotherhood under the influence of the fervent nationalist Maud Gonne, his lifelong friend and unrequited love. His best known poems are *The Lake Isle of Innisfree* and *Easter, 1916.* Yeats received Nobel Prize recognition for his writing one year after he was elected senator of the Irish Free State in 1922.

The Irish Literary Revival also produced the playwrights Jonathan Millington Synge and Sean O'Casey. A Dubliner, Synge spent time on the Aran Islands off the west coast of Ireland to study the Irish language and the ancient ways of the people. His plays *The Playboy of the Western World* and *The Tinker's Wedding* attempt to give a voice to the Irish peasantry, though many consider their language to be false and contrived. Productions of his dramas caused riots at the Abbey Theatre, where audiences found them offensive. O'Casey's working-class Dublin dramas, *Shadow of a Gunman* and *The Plough and the Stars* also brought uproar to the Abbey for their derisive view of militant nationalism.

The relationship that bound James Joyce to Dublin was tormented and complex. Though he abandoned the Ireland of his youth which he considered stifling and oppressive, it became the lifelong focus of his work. His novels include the largely autobiographical *Portrait of the Artist as a Young Man,* and *Ulysses,* in which he follows, in Greek-epic proportions, the wanderings of one Leopold Bloom throughout Dublin on June 16, 1904. Each year, a commemorative celebration of the day takes place with a "Bloomsday" stroll through the city that attracts crowds of enthusiasts. Joyce lived out his life in Paris, Trieste, Rome and Zurich, where he died in 1941.

48 top Seamus Heaney, the leading contemporary Irish poet and winner of the 1995 Nobel Prize for Literature, was born in County Derry in Northern Ireland in 1939. He now divides his time between Dublin and Harvard University.

48 bottom Jonathan Swift (1667–1745) was one of the first great Irish writers in the English language. For decades he presided as Dean over St. Patrick's Cathedral in Dublin, and he was one of the fiercest

critics of the inhumanity inflicted on Ireland by the English.

The plays of Samuel Beckett, who won the Nobel Prize for Literature in 1969, study absurd characters in search of the abstract. Born in Foxrock in 1906, he moved permanently to Paris in 1932, where he served for a short time as Joyce's secretary. His major works for the stage were written in French and translated into English and included *Waiting For Godot, Endgame* and *Krapp's Last Tape*.

Irish literature also includes a long list of additional authors, including Liam O'Flaherty, whose novels and short stories, including *The Informer*, reveal his devotion to the cause of Irish independence. The hilarious tales of Flann O'Brien hover between satire and fantasy, while the

plays of the quintessential Dubliner Brendan Behan, including *The Hostage,* are filled with black humour, bawdy celebration and stark politics. A militant nationalist, Behan was arrested as a youth for his IRA activities. His novel *The Borstal Boy* tells of his time in a reform prison in Britain. He died of alcoholism in 1964 at the age of forty-one.

Essential works for readers of Irish literature also include the short stories of Frank O'Connor and Sean O'Faolain; the novels of Elizabeth Bowen, Edna O'Brien and Roddy Doyle; the poetry of Brian Merriman, Patrick Kavanagh and Seamus Heaney; and the plays of Lady Gregory, Hugh Leonard, Tom Murphy and Brian Friel, though the list goes on.

50 top Trim Castle, one of the largest Anglo-Norman fortresses in the country, stands along the banks of the River Boyne in County Meath. The three-storey keep, surrounded by a curtain wall 11 feet thick, was raised in 1220 on the site of the original wooden motte-and-bailey built here by Hugh de Lacy in 1172.

50-51 The Rock of Cashel in County Tipperary was the seat of the kings of Munster until the end of the 11th century, when it was turned over to the Church. The present remains of the fortress are all ecclesiastical, including the Cathedral, the round tower and the Hiberno-Romanesque Cormac's Chapel.

Lismore, Dunluce, Askeaton, Glenquin—the names of Irish castles conjure up storybook fantasy. Yet their history is far more violent than romantic. Visions of lords and ladies quickly fade before the brutal images of medieval warfare, when attacking enemies were often subdued by the dropping of burning oil from the parapets. And actually, many of the grandiose structures, though dubbed castles, are, technically speaking, tower-houses or fortified residences which sequestered a despised invader. But, whatever the nomenclature, these castellated edifices represent an architectural and historical treasury in the inventory of Irish national monuments.

The first castles in Ireland were built by the Anglo-Normans from which to subjugate the Irish after the 1169 invasion. Originally wooden motte-and-bailey structures, the construction of Norman castles evolved within a few decades into massive stone keeps—usually square or rectangular structures topped with battlemented parapets and surrounded by a stone curtain wall of defence. The motte-and-baileys consisted of a wooden tower built on a mound (motte) of earth, which was surrounded by a deep ditch containing ramparts of heavy timber. Another barricaded trench formed the bailey, or enclosure for the outer buildings such as stables and barracks. The motte-and-baileys were assembled quickly, but their vulnerability to fire prompted the introduction of their stone successors.

By the fifteenth century the persistent Gaelic threat to the Anglo-Normans obliged them to construct defensive tower-house residencies that were a crude version of the

51 top Blarney Castle in County Cork is a 15th-century tower-house built by Cormac MacCarthy. The fortress is popular with visitors because of the Blarney Stone which sits at the base of one of the

battlements; kissing the stone is said to endow eloquence. The legend dates back to the time of Elizabeth I, whose demands were repeatedly avoided by the glib speech of the smooth-talking MacCarthy.

51 bottom Bunratty Castle in County Clare, the seat of the O'Briens, lords of Thomond, was built in the 15th century on the site of a number of earlier structures. The tower-house was bought and restored by Lord Gort in the 1950s, and then turned over to the state. Medieval banquets are held for tourists in the castle, and the attached "folk park" is an outdoor museum of traditional rural life in Ireland.

52-53 In 1832, the second Earl of Dunraven built Adare Manor on the site of a 13th-century Norman castle near the lovely village of Adare in County Limerick. The neo-Gothic manor house is now a luxurious hotel surrounded by 1,000 acres of parks and a golf course.

manor house, built with security rather than aesthetics in mind. Three to five storeys high with a notched parapet, they also featured a curtain wall enclosing a bawn, for the safekeeping of cattle and sheep.

A splendid example of medieval castle architecture is found at Trim, County Meath. This thirteenth-century, three-storey keep was completed in 1220 and replacing the motte-and-bailey erected in 1172 on the same site. One of the most impressive stone fortresses in Ireland, Trim Castle boasts walls which are 11 feet thick. The River Boyne runs along one side, while the remaining three sides were originally bordered by a drawbridged moat.

Also on the site of an original motte-and-bailey that was replaced with a stone structure, Bunratty Castle in County Clare was destroyed several times before the surviving fifteenth-century tower-house was erected. In Irish hands for 300 years, mainly under the McNamaras and the O'Briens, the castle was finally handed over to Cromwell's army. Purchased by Lord Gort in 1956, it was carefully restored and furnished with authentic period pieces. As part of the greater Bunratty Castle and Folk Park, nightly medieval banquets are held for tourists in the ancient tower, while the folk park houses a replica village recalling 19th-century rural life in Ireland.

The castle of Knappoguea—a nearby fifteenth-century castle fortress of the McNamara clan—is also a theatre for medieval banquets, as is the 16th-century Dunguaire Castle, a

54 top Kilkea Castle in Castledermot near Athy, County Kildare, now an elegant hotel, once belonged to the Fitz-Geralds, Earls of Kildare. An Anglo-Norman fortress built in 1180, the luxurious castle is reputed to be haunted by the ghost of Gerard, the eleventh Lord of Kildare.

54 bottom Aughnanure Castle stands on the shores of Lough Corrib in County Galway. Its imposing six-storey keep provides a wonderful observation point for the beautiful surroundings. The tower was built in 1500 by the O'Flahertys, the fiercest clan in the region.

54-55 The 16th-century Dunguaire Castle sits on Kinvara Bay in County Galway. The massive, intact keep is located just a few miles from the picturesque village of Kinvara.

55 top Kilkenny Castle, rebuilt and expanded in various styles over the centuries, was the seat of the Butlers from the 14th century until 1935. It sits on the site of the motte-and-bailey built by the Anglo-Norman invader Strongbow in 1172.

56-57 Nearly destroyed by fire in 1823, the 17th-century keep of Birr Castle in County Offaly was rebuilt and restored in neo-Gothic style. The castle occupies the site of a medieval fortress of the O'Carroll clan, and is still occupied by the Earls of Rosse. The interior holds a rich collection of period furniture, including a Celtic harp and a console table, the base of which features a wood-carved coat of arms. Outside is a gigantic telescope, built for William Parsons, the third Earl of Rosse, in 1845. The demesne, which is open to the public, also contains exquisite gardens and walkways.

sentinel set on a rocky spur overlooking Kinvara Bay. In Counties Limerick and Clare, along the Shannon estuary, are a string of castles including the ruins of the medieval strongholds of the Desmond FitzGeralds at Askeaton and Shanid, and the heavily restored Castle Matrix, a former Desmond tower-house which was confiscated by Elizabeth I. In their youth, Edmund Spenser and Walter Raleigh often met here to revel in their loathing of the native Irish. Several miles away is Glenquin Castle, a modern restoration of a seven-storey tower-house.

The Anglo-Norman invader Strongbow built a motte-and-bailey on the site of Kilkenny Castle in 1172, of which no trace remains. His son-in-law erected the original stone fortress here, which lent its groundplan to the present building. The Butler family, earls of Ormond, kept possession of Kilkenny Castle from the end of the fourteenth century until 1935. The structure was remodeled by Ormond descendents several times, and completely rebuilt in the nineteenth century.

The Rock of Cashel in County Tipperary—a giant circular mound which rises 200 feet above the surrounding plain—served as the seat of the kings of Munster, including Brian Boru, from the fifth to the eleventh centuries. It was then handed over to the Church, and all the present remains are monastic. The cluster of adjoining buildings that make up the ecclesiastical fortress include a cathedral, a Romanesque chapel, a round tower and an archbishop's castle.

Built by Cormac MacCarthy in 1127, Cormac's Chapel is a two-chambered church with typically Irish high-pitched roofs. The fine

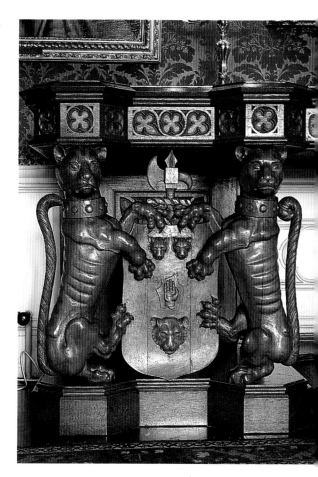

58-59 Ashford Castle, in a splendid setting on Lough Corrib in County Mayo, was largely constructed over a thirty-year period in the 1800s by Sir Arthur Edward Guinness, later Lord Ardilaun. Its battlemented façade incorporates the remains of the 13th-century Norman castle of the de Burgos and the 18th-century chateau Ashford House, built by the Oranmore and Browne families. The luxurious hotel has played host to many heads of state, including President Reagan who stayed there in 1984. The grounds of the castle contains beautiful lawns, gardens, and a golf course. Dotted with small islands, the adjoining Lough Corrib is an angler's paradise. Scottish bagpipes may be heard during hotel parties, as they may have been in days of old, when Anglo-Irish nobility gathered for festivities.

tympanums of the main doorways are splendidly sculpted, and inside the chapel is a twelfth-century stone sarcophagus carved in the Scandinavian style. The north trancept of the fifteenth-century cathedral contains a number of finely sculptured tombs depicting the Apostles and other saints. Spiral staircases run up to the central tower, leading to a series of defensive passageways that are also linked to the twelfth-century round tower at the northeast corner of the cathedral.

Not far from Cashel is the small town of Cahir (from the Irish *cathair,* fortress), with one of the largest medieval castles in Ireland. A high rectangular keep, Cahir Castle was originally built in the thirteenth century, greatly enlarged over the next two hundred years and repeatedly restored in modern times. Dramatically situated on a rocky islet overlooking the River Suir, this massive and well-preserved limestone structure made an excellent location for such films as *Excalibur* and *Barry Lyndon.*

A few miles northeast of Cork is Blarney Castle, perhaps the most famous of Ireland's tower-houses. The imposing four-storey fortress is perched on a spur of rock overlooking the River Martin. It was the fifteenth-century castle of the MacCarthy clan, where Cormac MacCarthy, Earl of Blarney, composed such deft rhetoric against Queen Elizabeth's demands for taxes and fealty that he was able to elude her requests. Since then, "blarney" has become a colloquial expression for Irish verbosity, and kissing under a stone at the base of one of the battlements is said to endow eloquence.

Irish castles are scattered throughout the land, inviting visitors to make endless new discoveries. In Connemara, one can thrill to the twelfth-century remains of Castle Kirke which are nestled on a little wooded islet in Ballynahinch Lough. Outside of Galway near Oughterard, Aughnanure Castle was built by the O'Flahertys at the end of the fifteenth century. The six-storey tower-house can be climbed to the roof for a

spectacular view of Lough Corrib.

Perhaps the most evocative ruins on the island are those of Dunluce Castle in County Antrim. The ruins of this medieval fortress sit dramatically on a cliff of a rocky island connected to the mainland by a bridge. Some say that the castle was abandoned, while others declare that several servants were lost when, during a storm in 1639, part of the kitchen collapsed into a cave.

Great neo-Gothic mansions and "castles" built in the nineteenth century, such as Adare Manor in County Limerick, Ashford Castle in County Mayo, and Dromoland Castle in County Clare, have been transformed into some of Ireland's most spectacular hotels. The second Lord Dunraven built Adare Manor close to the ruins of a thirteenth-century Desmond castle, while Dromoland Castle was built on the site of a sixteenth-century fortress of the O'Brien clan. Some of the enormous profits of the Guinness Brewery went into the construction of Ashford Castle, which was built for Arthur Guinness in 1870 and is now the most luxurious hotel on the island.

Another example of a nineteenth-century, neo-Gothic castle is located at Lismore, County Waterford. Erected from the shell of the seventeenth-century castle of Richard Boyle, Earl of Cork, the current structure also sits on the site of a twelfth-century stronghold of King John. Lismore Castle is a vast, turreted edifice surrounded by splendid gardens and perched atop a wooded crag overhanging the River Blackwater. Robert Boyle, son of Lord Cork, was born in the castle, and later went on to formulate Boyle's Law and be hailed as the "father of modern chemistry."

62 top Set on the banks of the River Suir in County Tipperary, Holy Cross Abbey was founded in 1180 by Cistercian monks and rebuilt in the 15th century. Careful and extensive reconstruction in 1975 has fully restored the medieval church and its cloister. The abbey houses what are said to be two precious fragments of the True Cross and thus are the annual destination for thousands of pilgrims. The chancel, transepts and crossing are exquisitely vaulted, and the ribbed vault and twisted columns of the original shrine of the Crucifixion relics are extraordinary.

62-63 The ruins of the 13th-century Franciscan friary of Timoleague in County Cork were once one of Ireland's largest religious centres. Built on the site of an original monastery established by St. Molaga in the 6th century, Timoleague (Tigh Molaige, "house of Molaga") is located near the estuary of the River Argideen in the far southeast of the country.

One does not have to be religious to succumb to the allure of Ireland's monasteries. As much havens of scholarship as abstention, they were often situated in wild, remote and breathtakingly beautiful settings, and were retreats devoted to the preservation and dissemination of higher knowledge and the execution of exquisite decorative arts.

Contacts with Britain and France, mainly through trade, brought Christianity to Ireland by the beginning of the fifth century. There were already enough Christians on the island for the Pope to send them their first bishop, Palladius, in A.D. 431, one year before St. Patrick's legendary conversion of the country.

Though Patrick and his co-evangelists attempted a Christian-ization of Ireland based upon a European diocesan hierarchy, the townless, tribal nature of Gaelic society favoured a monastic system. While the Gaels' respect for art and learning attracted them to the monastic life, the church that developed in these settlements tolerated—and often assimilated—the native pagan customs. Thus, the fusion of the new religion with the ethics and traditions of the existing Gaelic social structure created a distinctly Irish form of Early Christianity.

As the early monastic sites were established, the popularity of the ascetic life grew rapidly, with a virtual explosion in the number of monks on the island. The thriving centres of learning lured many visitors, including students and Christian scholars from abroad escaping the Dark Ages. More and more lay members of the society also settled near and even within the monasteries, many of which eventually evolved into true monastic cities.

The monks produced the first written words in Ireland (in Latin, in Irish, and often in a combination of the two) and it was they who were the first to record the early Gaelic sagas and folktales that had been handed down orally for centuries. While the rest of Europe regressed during the Dark Ages, the Irish monasteries revelled in a golden age of art and literacy (A.D. 500–1100). But while scribes and artisans reached new heights of glory with their manuscripts and metalwork, the strict religious order intended for Christian monastic life was often loosely reinterpreted, or virtually abandoned.

Abbots were often members of the laity who inherited their office by

63 top left The imposing ruins of Boyle Abbey in County Roscommon are the finest and best-preserved example of an Irish Cistercian house of the 12th century, and include the church, sacristy, cloister and monks' cells. Founded in 1161, Boyle Abbey survived many sieges and attacks, and was active as an abbey until the 16th century.

63 top right Sheep grazing in a meadow near the extensive remains of the Augustinian priory at the village of Kells, County Kilkenny (not to be confused with Kells Monastery in County Meath). Founded in 1193, the present ruins date from the 14th and 15th centuries. Three of the five square towers which were incorporated into the outer wall for protection are visible here, and give the ruins a fortress-like quality.

right of family succession. Many priests were married, while divorce, concubinage, and polygamy were common in the society as a whole. The monks and priests were inclined to merge their new spirituality with ancient pre-Christian rites, relying on magic and potions as well as the hand of God. By the twelfth century, the corruption of power and lack of religious discipline in the monasteries led ecclesiastical hierarchy to intervene, resulting in a complete reorganization of the church in Ireland. New monastic orders were introduced from abroad as the European diocesan system replaced the old monastic network. The magnificent abbeys of the Cistercians and the Augustinians were established at this time, the splendid remains of which may be viewed throughout the country today.

While the buildings in the early monasteries were very small and functional, more elaborate ecclesiastical construction began in the eleventh century, when Irish-Romanesque or "Hiberno-Romanesque" building and decorative carving were introduced. The characteristics of Romanesque architecture are rounded windows, doors and arches and massive of structure. The particularly Irish version of the style used exceedingly elaborate carvings—complex geometric, zigzag, and interlaced designs, complemented by exotic flora and fauna motifs and fantastic variations of the human form.

A monastic tour of Ireland can begin right outside of Dublin, in County Meath. Ten miles from Navan in the valley of the River Blackwater is Kells Monastery, founded by St. Columba (or St. Columbcille) in the sixth century. Most of the buildings here date from the relocation of monks from another of Columba's monasteries, on Iona off the coast of Scotland; in A.D. 804 they were driven out by Viking raids on their settlement. Though it is not known where the Book of Kells was transcribed and illuminated, it was preserved here until being brought to Trinity College in Dublin for safekeeping during the Cromwellian wars. The remains of the monastic site include St. Columba's House, an oratory with a steeply pitched stone roof and exceptionally thick walls, a round tower and several richly ornamented high crosses.

To the east, outside of Drogheda in County Louth, is Mellifont Abbey which was founded in 1142 by St. Malachy. It was the earliest Cistercian abbey in Ireland, of which only scant, yet interesting ruins remain—in particular the octagonal fountain house. Following the dissolution of the monasteries by Henry VIII in 1539, the property was confiscated by the English. In 1603 they chose Mellifont as the site for the signing of the treaty between Hugh O'Neill and Lord Mountjoy ending the Nine Years' War. Nearby is Monasterboice, established in the sixth century by St.

Boyce. The site contains some of the finest and best-preserved Early Christian relics in the country, including the Cross of Muiredach.

Just south of Dublin, in the heart of the Wicklow Mountains, is Glendalough ("glen of the two lakes"). Seeking tranquillity and solitude, St. Kevin came here to live as a hermit in the sixth century. A descendent of the royal house of Leinster, legend has it that Kevin's good looks were so tempting to women that he was forced to retire from natural society. The monastery he founded there remained active until the thirteenth century, the ruins of which extend for two miles along the lakes. The cluster of buildings around the Lower Lake include four churches, a cathedral and the Priest's House. A round tower stands in the centre of the settlement, beyond which two more churches and "St. Kevin's Cell" are found along the Upper Lake.

To the south in County Kilkenny, is one of the most intact monastic ruins in Ireland at Jerpoint Abbey. Established in 1180 by the Cistercians, one can still see the original church and cloister with their outstanding Romanesque sculptures. A lesser-known Cistercian house founded in the same year is Holy Cross Abbey, located just south of Thurles in County Tipperary. The monks here were said to possess a piece of the True Cross which attracted many pilgrims and gave the abbey its name.

One of the finest early monastic sites in all of Europe is found at Skellig Michael (Sceiligh Micheál) on a rocky island peak eight miles off the coast of Kerry's Iveragh Peninsula. On a ledge 700 feet above the sea sit the tiny, ancient structures–six beehive cells (clocháin) and two oratories—which remain intact today. Built from drystone (without mortar), the precisely laid stones are corbelled (inwardly overlapped) to shape the roofs—rounded on the beehive dwellings and steeply-pitched on the oratory chapels. The site is accessed by climbing over 600 steps hewn from the rock. (To reach the island, guided boat tours may be arranged at Valentia Island, weather permitting.)

Further north on the Dingle Peninsula, beehive huts are found at Cahir Murphy on the road to Slea Head, while not far away at Ballydavid, the seventh- or eighth-century Gallarus Oratory can be seen. The best preserved of all of these Early Christian structures, this rectangular oratory measures ten by fifteen feet, with walls over three feet thick. Shaped like an upturned boat, its meticulous construction has left it watertight after 1,200 years.

Brandon Bay on the northern coast of the peninsula is where St. Brendan, (Brendan the Navigator) is said to have set off on his sixth-century voyages to North America. Whether these journeys are legend or fact is unknown, but we do know the

68-69 *The origins of the Kilmacduagh Monastery are steeped in legend. A son had been born to the proud King of Connaught, who heard a prophesy that a son to be born to a woman named Rhinach would exceed the king's offspring in greatness. In a jealous rage, he ordered Rhinach to be killed. She was thrown into a lake with a rock tied to her neck, but miraculously survived and gave birth to Colman MacDuagh. When the king's son, Guaire, became king himself, he found Colman living as a hermit at Kilmacduagh and built a fine monastery for him, to make amends for his father's evil deed.*

68 top and 69 bottom right Sligo Abbey was founded by Maurice FitzGerald in 1253 as a Dominican friary. The complex was rebuilt after being seriously damaged by fire in 1414 and was *devastated again by Cromwell's troops in the 1600s. The well-preserved remains of the friary include the original 13th-century church choir with lancet windows, and the 15th-century nave and finely carved altar.*

69 top right In a cemetery in the small village of Ahenny, County Tipperary, stand two 8th- or 9th-century high crosses, perhaps the earliest in Ireland. The South Cross shown is carved with interlace and spirals, bordered by a rope-like edging and embossed with five protuberances reminiscent of the studs in the decorative metalwork of the era.

saint founded a monastery at Ardfert, situated north of Tralee in County Kerry, in the sixth century. The monastic remains here all date to the thirteenth century, including the majestic ruins of St. Brendan's Cathedral, the little Romanesque church of Temple na Hoe, and the ruins of a Franciscan Friary a few hundred yards away.

Another of Brendan's ancient monastic settlements, dating from A.D. 563, is found at Clonfert in County Galway. The west doorway of the twelfth-century Cathedral here is a masterpiece of Irish Romanesque sculpture. Also in County Galway near Gort is Kilmacduagh Monastery, with a cathedral and several churches dating from the twelfth century. While the settlement boasts the one of the tallest round towers in Ireland, the structure lists a full two feet off centre, reminiscent of the Leaning Tower of Pisa.

In the northwest, the remains of the Augustinian abbey at Ballintubber, just south of Castlebar in County Mayo, include a Romanesque church and a Gothic cloister. Despite the devastation wrought by Cromwell's army in 1653, Ballintubber has remained a continuously active religious centre since its founding in 1216.

Sacred sites in Ireland are often found in unexpected places. On the Aran Islands off the coast of County Clare, which are riddled with prehistoric forts and ancient remains,

70 top The monastery of Clonmacnoise, beside the River Shannon in County Offaly, was founded by St. Ciarán in the 6th century. It grew into Ireland's greatest centre of medieval Christianity, learning and art, and one of the most famous seats of monastic study in Europe. Splendid illuminated manuscripts were created here, as well as exquisitely forged religious ornaments such as the Cross of Clonmacnoise (now at the National Museum in Dublin). Clonmacnoise was once the burial place of high-kings, including Rory O'Connor. Throughout the centuries, the monastery was subjected to many attacks by warring Irish tribes, Vikings, and Normans, until the English finally destroyed it in 1552. The remains include a cathedral, seven churches, two round towers, several spectacular high crosses and hundreds of graveslabs.

71 left Among the most fascinating remains at Clonmacnoise is the thousand-year-old Cross of the Scriptures, one of the finest high crosses in Ireland. It dates from the 9th or 10th century and bears the inscription: "A prayer for Colman, who made this cross for King Flann," an indication that the cross was commissioned by, or erected on the tomb of, Flann mac Mael Sechnaill, a royal patron of the monastery who died in A.D. 918. On the west face of the cross shown here, the central Crucifixion scene is complemented by carvings of the Passion of Christ.

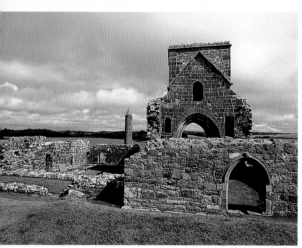

70 bottom On Devenish Island in Lower Lough Erne, two miles from Enniskillen in the lakelands of County Fermanagh, are the ruins of the most important monastic complex in Northern Ireland. Founded in the 6th century by St. Molaise, the site is dominated by a perfectly preserved, 12th-century round tower. The ecclesiastical buildings include the small and primitive Teampull Mór (Great Church) dating from the 13th century, St. Molaise's House, a 12th-century windowless cell, and St. Mary's Priory, a 15th-century church built for the Augustinians.

visitors to the largest of the three islands, Inishmore (boat from Galway City), may see one of the smallest churches in the world, Teampall Bheanáin (St. Benan's Church) as well as the last remnant of St. Enda's monastic settlement, Tighlagh Enda. On the smallest island, Innisheer (boat from Doolin in County Clare), the tiny St. Cavan's Church is cleared of the huge drifts of sand that nearly bury it each year by islanders celebrating the saint's feast day on June 14.

Island monasteries are also found on Scattery Island in County Clare (boats from Cappagh Pier near Kilrush) and the island of Innismurray in County Sligo (boat from Streedagh). St. Senan founded the settlement on Scattery in the sixth century, which includes the ruins of five churches and a round tower. Of great significance in its day, the monastery was destroyed during the reign of Elizabeth I. The monastic establishment on the island of Innismurray was founded by St. Molaise in the early sixth century. Here are found the remains of three churches and a beehive hut, all surrounded by an enormous drystone wall.

Boyle Abbey, a Cistercian house founded by monks from Mellifont in 1161, is located in County Roscommon. Though roofless, the nave, choir and transepts survive on the church and reveal the richness of Cistercian architecture and ornamentation.

The famous monastery of Clonmacnoise on the banks of the Shannon in County Offaly was founded by St. Ciarán in A.D. 548. The ruins scattered amid the fields are the remains of what was once one of the richest and most celebrated centres of learning and art in Europe. Here, precious objects were crafted with extraordinary skill, such as the Cross of Clonmacnoise that is now on view at the National Museum in Dublin. The magnificent ruins include over 200 Early Christian grave slabs, O'Rourke's Tower, several churches, the Cathedral, additional high crosses, and the ruins of a castle. Valuable manuscripts were produced here, including the Book of the Dun Cow, as well as many fine crosiers and reliquaries. The settlement was raided by Vikings, attacked by the Normans and eventually devastated by Cromwell's army.

Since most of the monasteries in Ireland were besieged in a similar fashion, what remains of these Early Christian temples of scholarship and art are truly remarkable.

71 top right In a scenic corner of Connemara near Letterfrack in County Galway, Kylemore Abbey sits at the foot of a steep, wooded hillside on the shores of one of the three Kylemore Loughs. The castellated, neo-Gothic mansion, built by the British M. P. Mitchell Henry in 1864, is now a Benedictine convent. Its forested backdrop and reflected image in the lake creates a fairytale setting.

71 bottom right
Clonfert Cathedral,
south of Ballinasloe
in County Galway,
was built in 1200
and stands on the site
of an original
monastery founded
by St. Brendan the
Navigator in A.D. 563.
The west portal of the
cathedral is a
masterpiece of
Hiberno-
Romanesque design,
particularly the
gruesomely
intriguing
triangular pattern
of human heads on
the tympanum.
Within the church,
the chancel arch is
carved with fine
relief figures of angels
and a mermaid
holding a mirror.

72 top Coulagh Bay, one of the many Atlantic inlets on the Beara Peninsula in County Cork, is located between Bantry Bay and the Kenmare River. Beara is a scenic stretch of wild beauty, crowned by the Caha Mountains.

72-73 and 73 top left The rolling hills and green fields of Kerry's Iveragh Peninsula. The circuitous tour around the peninsula is called the Ring of Kerry, and comprises 90 miles of scenic roads from Killarney south to Kenmare, through Parknasilla, Waterville, Cahirciveen, Glenbeigh and Killorglin. The mainly coastal route traces the Atlantic shores of Ballinskelligs, St. Finan's and Dingle Bays, rising inland to mountains, mirror lakes and extraordinary landscapes.

Splendid, pastoral, wild, gentle, boisterous, solitary: the adjectives used to describe the physical Ireland are often contradictory, but never inaccurate. In a land of contrast and extremes, the natural offerings range from comforting pastures to rugged cliffs, from tranquil lakes to desolate weather-beaten outposts.

Visitors to Ireland are continually overwhelmed by the astounding natural beauty that unfolds throughout the island. Only minutes outside of the cities, open space and quiet refuge embrace the spirit, as mountains, lakes, meadows and beaches invite the mind to abandon concern, and the body to surrender to the sounds, the smells and the serenity of the land.

Beginning in the southwest, County Kerry's three peninsulas offer some of the most spectacular and varied scenery in the country. Shared by the counties of Cork and Kerry, the Beara Peninsula is a virtual mountain in the sea. The Caha and Slieve Miskish ranges give it its form, while its wild beauty is adorned with lakes, waterfalls and moors of flowering heather. A symphony of haunting beauty is created by its craggy rocks as they are pounded by the sea beneath a shroud of mist.

The larger Iveragh Peninsula is a succession of surprisingly rugged landscapes, lush vegetation and stunning lakes that make up that special itinerary known as the Ring of Kerry. Travelling west from Kenmare at the southern end of the coastal circuit, the gentle landscape along the bay of the Atlantic known as the River Kenmare is densely covered with the area's exotic flora that includes rhododendrons, palms and giant ferns. Originally imported to the area as an ornamental, the purple-flowering rhododendron has thrived in the area's subtropical climate, a gift of the warm breezes of the Gulf Stream. The species has now spread so wildly as to threaten the woods of the indigenous oak. Beyond Caherdaniel, at Derrynane National Park, even fig trees grow in the balmy temperatures.

Off the coast of the western end of the peninsula, the small Skellig Islands rise out of the sea as sheer pinnacles. Great Skellig (or Skellig Michael) is known for its ancient monastery, while Little Skellig is an inaccessible ornithological reserve inhabited by tens of thousands of seabirds, especially gannets, whose six-foot wingspan is displayed as they soar from their nests and suddenly

73 top right Off the western coast of the Iveragh Peninsula and connected by bridge to the mainland, Valentia Island is the site of one of the most important weather stations in Europe. The Heritage Centre hosts "The Skellig Experience" exhibit, which informs visitors on the marine bird life of the offshore Skellig and Puffin Islands and provides a simulated, audio-visual tour of the ancient monastery on Skellig Michael.

74-75 Grazing sheep and hedgerows of blooming yellow gorse adorn a vista of green fields in County Waterford.

The variety of landscapes in the area include mountain slopes, tranquil lakes and river ports.

Waterford's Atlantic coast is graced with gentle beaches and rocky peninsulas.

plunge in vertical dives for fish. The tiny Puffin Island to the north is sanctuary to the thousands of birds that give the island its name, as well as storm petrels, razorbills and shearwaters. Varied vistas of rocky slope, heathered hills, lakes, rivers and vast ocean may be seen from the coast road, which climbs numerous mountain gaps and drops down to the many bays and beaches of the Atlantic. An abundance of fish make sea and freshwater fishing a significant activity on the peninsula, and the salmon and trout-filled loughs and rivers are a particular attraction.

The road from Cahirciveen to Glenbeigh is one of spectacular scenery, hugging the steep hills to provide gorgeous views across Dingle

Bay to the rough peaks of the Dingle Peninsula. Inland from Kilorglin are the majestic Macgillicuddy's Reeks, a range of red sandstone peaks including the highest summit in Ireland at Carrantuohill (3,414 feet). Climbing in these mountains will reward the strenuous with stunning views of the lakes of Killarney: Lough Leane, Muckross Lough, Upper Lake and Lough Guitane. Some of the most exquisite glacially forged scenery in the country may be seen in a tour around this district, highlighted by a journey through the dramatic Gap of Dunloe, a wild gorge between Macgillicuddy's Reeks and the Purple Mountains. Wooded islets dot the loughs, whose shores are densely wooded with oak, bamboo and fern. In summer, foxgloves bloom along the roads while huge rhododendrons wind their way up into the hills.

The shoals and beaches of Dingle, the next peninsula to the north, stretch on endlessly beneath impressive mountains and remarkable cliffs. The roads are edged with hedgerows of fuschia, while the stone cottages and irregular fields are enclosed by miles of low dry-stone

76-77 Off the coast of Kerry, Great Skellig (Skellig Michael), Little Skellig (centre left), and Puffin Islands (bottom left) are protected marine bird sanctuaries. Puffins (top right), razorbills (top left), and gannets (page 77) thrive in these ornithological refuges.

78-79 A field of sunflowers reflects the setting sun near Sybil Point, a rocky promontory that juts out over Smerwick Harbour on the Dingle Peninsula. A land of sandy beaches, coastal cliffs and rolling fields, the northwestern end of the Dingle Peninsula is a natural paradise.

walls running down to the sea. Dingle is the Ireland of imagination, the Ireland of films such as *Ryan's Daughter* which was shot here at the little village of Dunquin. Over two miles of untouched sandy beach are found at Inch, the romantic setting for several powerful sequences in the movie. Beyond the sheltered harbour of Dingle town lie the westernmost cliffs of Slea Head, which offer a breathtaking view of the Blasket Islands (unihabited since 1953). This treacherous shore has witnessed many shipwrecks, including two vessels of the Spanish Armada in the sixteenth century and a cargo ship as recently as 1982. The highest point on the peninsula is Mount Brandon (3,085 feet), part of a range of mountains that plummet 2,000 feet into the sea

at Brandon Head. The inland road from Dingle town to Cloghane passes over the rugged gorges of the Connor Pass through the middle of the peninsula.

The small farms of northwest County Clare, between Lisdoonvarna and Ballyvaughan, suddenly give way to the strange rocky land of the Burren (*boirinn*, Gaelic for "great rock"), an almost eerie and unearthly landscape—virtual sloping fields of stone. These barren tables of rock are formed by fissured limestone or *karst*. Though seemingly hostile to life forms, a surprising variety of small plants and alpine wildflowers, including tiny orchids and gentian are found within the deep crevices of the "pavements." Beneath the grey plateau of rock is an extraordinary network of underground streams, caves and "potholes," while seasonal ponds on the surface, known as "turloughs," disappear in dry weather.

Several miles away, the Cliffs of Moher, perhaps the most spectacular sight in Ireland, stand majestically over the Atlantic. Rising vertically out of the sea, the sheer precipices run along five miles of coastline and range in height from 400 to 650 feet. Below, individual rocky pinnacles protrude from the thundering surf. Stratified layers of rock can be perceived in the cliff face, which is inhabited by many species of seabirds, including puffins.

Across the water are the Aran Islands, whose topography is similar to that of the limestone-imbedded Burren. The three islands of this *Gaeltacht* (Irish-speaking) chain include the largest, Inishmore, the middle island of Inishmaan and the smallest, Inisheer. The islanders have struggled for centuries to clear the rugged, infertile land of rock. With successive layering of sand and seaweed, they have created small

"garden" fields, providing soil for their crops. Tiny fields enclosed by high drystone walls predominate the landscape, and the narrow roadways slope down to white sand beaches, secluded coves and, on the higher sides of Inishmaan and Inisheer, great slabbed cliffs of limestone that drop dramatically to the sea. (Inishmore is reached by ferry from Galway, by boat from Rossaveal, or by plane from Connemara Airport; the other two islands are serviced by inter-island ferry. Inisheer is also accessible by boat from Doolin Pier in County Clare.)

Fishing has always been a mainstay of life, and islanders brave the rough seas in *curraghs*, traditional canoes constructed of wooden lath and covered with tarred canvas stretched over the hull. The wild Atlantic currents, especially in storms, have claimed many fishermen's lives over the years, and until recent decades, kept the islands virtually isolated from the mainland.

All of the islands are littered with antiquities, but Dún Aenghus on Inishmore is the most spectacular. One of the finest prehistoric forts in Europe, it consists of three semi-circular rings of stone wall, with an additional outer defence of thousands of sharp-headed pillar stones. Sitting on the edge of a sheer cliff that rises 300 feet from the Atlantic, the magnificent site and the view of the sea beyond is breathtaking.

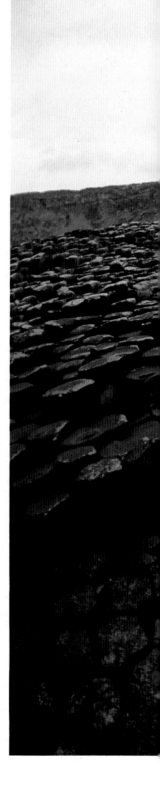

82-83 and 83 top Giant's Causeway on the coast of County Antrim is the most spectacular natural curiosity in all of Ireland. A massive grouping of 37,000 erect, hexagonal columns of basalt in heights ranging from a few inches to 80 feet are joined to form a terrain of steps,

platforms and towering edifices. The natural phenomenon is a result of an underground explosion that took place approximately 60 million years ago. As the boiling lava surfaced and cooled, the basalt mass crystallized, creating the extraordinary column formations.

84-85 A stretch of
pristine, sandy beach
on the shores of
County Donegal,
part of the wild and
unspoiled coastline of
this northwest region
which includes
mountainous cliffs,
windswept headlands
and spectacular
seascapes.

84 bottom A typical
scene along the shores
of Connemara, a
wild and rocky
bogland crowned by
the peaks of the
Twelve Pins and
bordered by the
Atlantic coastline of
coves and quiet inlets.

85 top right Modern
thatched cottages in
"holiday villages" are
available for rental
by tourists in several
Irish coastal regions.

85 lower right Ireland
is a golfer's paradise,
with nearly 300 courses
throughout the island,
in idyllic settings
surrounded by
spectacular scenery.

County Galway's western region, known as Connemara—bordered by Lough Corrib on the east and the Atlantic coast on the south and west—is a sparsely populated area of rocky land, brown bog, purple lakes and steel-blue sea. Crowned by the peaks of the Maamturk Mountains and the Twelve Pins, the topography of the valleys ranges from the rocky "lunar landscapes" around Spiddal to the lough-filled valleys near Recess and Leenane, all interspersed with immense stretches of bogland. Stretches of unspoiled sandy beach are often found amid the rocky inlets of the indented shoreline, while hikers will enjoy isolated terrain in every direction. Sheep cover the hills, donkeys cart backpacks of turf and seaweed and Connemara ponies wander the roads in pursuit of good patches for grazing. The angling centre of Cashel Bay is a quiet corner of green, beyond which the mountain roads lead to the shores of Ballynahinch Lake and eventually Clifden, the "capital of Connemara."

The County of Mayo has a fantastic Atlantic coastline, with miles of beautiful, empty beaches near Louisburgh. Off the coast are the islands of Inishturk, Inishbofin and Clare Island. Inishbofin (accessible by

boat from Cleggan) is endowed with rugged cliffs, sandy beaches and small peaceful lakes, as well as antiquities including prehistoric forts and monastic ruins. Sailing, fishing and an abundance of natural flora and fauna attract many visitors.

Further north, Achill Island is accessible by a bridge from the mainland. The largest of the islands off the Irish coast, it consists mainly of bogland and heathered moors with hills that rise to 2,200 feet, forming magnificent cliffs on the north and west coasts. Below the quartzite summit of Slievemore are the Seal Caves that can be reached by boat from Dugort. Keel Beach runs for two miles, ending at the Minaun Cliffs that fall 800 feet to the sea. Another gorgeous sandy beach is

85 bottom left
Connemara ponies
are a docile, hardy
breed that feed on the
short sea grasses
native to the region's
coastal terrain. Used
as workhorses for
centuries, today they
are also bred for
riding and
showjumping.

located on the road to Keem, from where the peak of Croaghaun (2,068 feet) rises above a four-mile stretch of cliffs with wonderful views of the Atlantic.

"Yeats Country" in County Sligo is home to the many loughs celebrated by the poet in his writings. Both Lough Gill ("lake beauty") which Yeats adored, and the setting of his most famous poem, *The Lake Isle of Innisfree*, are just a few miles from Sligo Town, in the land where he spent so much of his childhood. Sligo's Glencar Lough is fed by the River Diffreen which flows down from the Darty Mountains. The "wandering water" as Yeats dubbed it, tumbles down three waterfalls here, the most well-known of which is the "Stream Against the Height," so named because of the wind which pushes the water back up the falls.

Heading north past the flat-topped table mountain of Ben Bulben, the coastal route leads to Donegal, perhaps the wildest and most isolated county in the country. Passing to the northwestern area beyond Killybegs, the dramatic ocean cliffs of the Slieve League Mountains, rising to a spectacular 2,000 feet, can best be observed from high points around Teelin. Further north at The Rosses (*Na Rosa*, or the Headlands) between the villages of Dungloe and Gweedore, one can find true escape in an unspoiled region. One hundred and twenty tiny lakes dot this area alone, and the extremely jagged coast offers a continuous panorama of rocks and sea, peninsulas and islands, fjords and bays. Beyond on the Gweedore Headland is Bloody Foreland, named for the dark-red shade of its rockface at sunset.

Nine miles offshore to the north lies Tory Island (reached by boat from Meenlaragh), a barren, windswept reef of rock without even a single tree. The Gaeltacht outpost contains a round tower and a prehistoric fortress known as the legendary stronghold of Balor, the one-eyed Celtic god of darkness. "Wishing stones" at the centre of the island are reputed to have the power to destroy enemies.

86 The Powerscourt Waterfall is three miles south of the Powerscourt Gardens, the demesne of the estate in the Wicklow Mountains near Enniskerry. The highest falls in Ireland or Britain, they plunge down the face of sheer rock from a height of 400 feet.

87 Gentle pastures and rolling hills, dotted with grazing sheep and cows dominate the Irish landscape. Winding rivers, tranquil lakes and hedgerows of blooming gorse are typical sights throughout the country.

88-89 Two particularly verdant images at the edges of the Burren in County Clare. Although green pastures such as these can be found near the coast and along rivers and lakes, the heart of the region—between Lisdoonvarna and Ballyvaughan—is a desolate yet fascinating landscape of fissured limestone. In Irish, Burren (Boirinn) means "great rock," and the area is in fact an immense karstic plateau, supporting a population of small plants and wildflowers within its crevices.

Inland, the protected forest wilderness at Glenveagh National Park is home to the largest herd of red deer in Ireland. Across the northern coast, Horn Head rises as the most imposing of Donegal's headlands, 600 feet of dizzying height that provide a haven for seabirds. Continuing on to the Rosguill and Fanad Peninsulas, the barren rocky promontories, cliffs and fjord-like inlets finally lead to Malin Head, the northernmost tip of Ireland.

One of the true wonders of nature is found at Giant's Causeway on the northern coast of County Antrim. Here 37,000 erect hexagonal basalt columns appear to have been perfectly and purposefully tiled together to form steps, pathways and staggered platforms extending down into the sea. The columns range in height from a few inches to the enormous pillars of the amphitheatre grouping, which reach heights of up to 80 feet. The scientific theory for the phenomenon goes back to a geological event of 60 million years ago when lava cooled as it surfaced, causing the crystallization of the rock. But far more interesting is the mythological explanation that tells of the great love of the giant Fionn MacCumhaill (Finn MacCool) for a giantess who lived on the island of Staffa along the Scottish coast. In order to reach his beloved, he threw stepping stones across the sea.

From heights of up to 2,000 feet, the Mourne Mountains sweep down to the sea in County Down. The Cooley Peninsula of County Louth provides wonderful views down the coast to Clogherhead.

South of Dublin in County Wicklow, known as the "garden of Ireland," Glendalough Forest Park encompasses a lake valley surrounded by the wooded Wicklow Mountains and is best known for its monastic ruins. Near Enniskerry, the Powerscourt Waterfall is the highest falls in Ireland, at nearly 400 feet. To the south, the Avondale Forest Park boasts a fine preserve of exotic trees. The coastal counties of Wexford and Waterford are low and flat, with long stretches of sandy beach and the driest climate on the island.

The southwestern coast of County Cork from Kinsale to Glengarriff offers varied and stunning seascapes, from fine sandy beaches to wild and rugged shores. Among the many small islands off the coast are Sherkin Island with its lovely beaches and prolific wildlife, and Cape Clear Island, which abounds in marine birdlife and provides a fantastic view of the Fastnet Rock Lighthouse (both islands are reached by boat from Baltimore). There is a discreet charm about the less touristy areas of Schull and Durrus, and the pastoral landscapes and small bays of the Sheep's Head Peninsula—the most

90 The coast of County Clare offers a variety of landscapes. Near Kilkee, a beautiful sandy beach gives rise to the dramatic cliffs of Castle Point, which stand 300 feet over the sea.

91-92-93-94 One of the most spectacular sights in Ireland, the Cliffs of Moher in northwest County Clare run for five miles along the coast and rise vertically from the pounding Atlantic at heights of up to 650 feet. The cliffs are home to a variety of seabirds, including puffins, and on a clear day provide a breathtaking view of the Aran Islands and the coasts of Galway to the north and Clare and Kerry to the south.

located on the road to Keem, from where the peak of Croaghaun (2,068 feet) rises above a four-mile stretch of cliffs with wonderful views of the Atlantic.

"Yeats Country" in County Sligo is home to the many loughs celebrated by the poet in his writings. Both Lough Gill ("lake beauty") which Yeats adored, and the setting of his most famous poem, *The Lake Isle of Innisfree*, are just a few miles from Sligo Town, in the land where he spent so much of his childhood. Sligo's Glencar Lough is fed by the River Diffreen which flows down from the Darty Mountains. The "wandering water" as Yeats dubbed it, tumbles down three waterfalls here, the most well-known of which is the "Stream Against the Height," so named because of the wind which pushes the water back up the falls.

Heading north past the flat-topped table mountain of Ben Bulben, the coastal route leads to Donegal, perhaps the wildest and most isolated county in the country. Passing to the northwestern area beyond Killybegs, the dramatic ocean cliffs of the Slieve League Mountains, rising to a spectacular 2,000 feet, can best be observed from high points around Teelin. Further north at The Rosses (*Na Rosa*, or the Headlands) between the villages of Dungloe and Gweedore, one can find true escape in an unspoiled region. One hundred and twenty tiny lakes dot this area alone, and the extremely jagged coast offers a continuous panorama of rocks and sea, peninsulas and islands, fjords and bays. Beyond on the Gweedore Headland is Bloody Foreland, named for the dark- red shade of its rockface at sunset.

Nine miles offshore to the north lies Tory Island (reached by boat from Meenlaragh), a barren, windswept reef of rock without even a single tree. The Gaeltacht outpost contains a round tower and a prehistoric fortress known as the legendary stronghold of Balor, the one-eyed Celtic god of darkness. "Wishing stones" at the centre of the island are reputed to have the power to destroy enemies.

86 The Powerscourt Waterfall is three miles south of the Powerscourt Gardens, the demesne of the estate in the Wicklow Mountains near Enniskerry. The highest falls in Ireland or Britain, they plunge down the face of sheer rock from a height of 400 feet.

87 Gentle pastures and rolling hills, dotted with grazing sheep and cows dominate the Irish landscape. Winding rivers, tranquil lakes and hedgerows of blooming gorse are typical sights throughout the country.

85 top right Modern thatched cottages in "holiday villages" are available for rental by tourists in several Irish coastal regions.

85 lower right Ireland is a golfer's paradise, with nearly 300 courses throughout the island, in idyllic settings surrounded by spectacular scenery.

County Galway's western region, known as Connemara—bordered by Lough Corrib on the east and the Atlantic coast on the south and west—is a sparsely populated area of rocky land, brown bog, purple lakes and steel-blue sea. Crowned by the peaks of the Maamturk Mountains and the Twelve Pins, the topography of the valleys ranges from the rocky "lunar landscapes" around Spiddal to the lough-filled valleys near Recess and Leenane, all interspersed with immense stretches of bogland. Stretches of unspoiled sandy beach are often found amid the rocky inlets of the indented shoreline, while hikers will enjoy isolated terrain in every direction. Sheep cover the hills, donkeys cart backpacks of turf and seaweed and Connemara ponies wander the roads in pursuit of good patches for grazing. The angling centre of Cashel Bay is a quiet corner of green, beyond which the mountain roads lead to the shores of Ballynahinch Lake and eventually Clifden, the "capital of Connemara."

The County of Mayo has a fantastic Atlantic coastline, with miles of beautiful, empty beaches near Louisburgh. Off the coast are the islands of Inishturk, Inishbofin and Clare Island. Inishbofin (accessible by

boat from Cleggan) is endowed with rugged cliffs, sandy beaches and small peaceful lakes, as well as antiquities including prehistoric forts and monastic ruins. Sailing, fishing and an abundance of natural flora and fauna attract many visitors.

Further north, Achill Island is accessible by a bridge from the mainland. The largest of the islands off the Irish coast, it consists mainly of bogland and heathered moors with hills that rise to 2,200 feet, forming magnificent cliffs on the north and west coasts. Below the quartzite summit of Slievemore are the Seal Caves that can be reached by boat from Dugort. Keel Beach runs for two miles, ending at the Minaun Cliffs that fall 800 feet to the sea. Another gorgeous sandy beach is

85 bottom left Connemara ponies are a docile, hardy breed that feed on the short sea grasses native to the region's coastal terrain. Used as workhorses for centuries, today they are also bred for riding and showjumping.

Inland, the protected forest wilderness at Glenveagh National Park is home to the largest herd of red deer in Ireland. Across the northern coast, Horn Head rises as the most imposing of Donegal's headlands, 600 feet of dizzying height that provide a haven for seabirds. Continuing on to the Rosguill and Fanad Peninsulas, the barren rocky promontories, cliffs and fjord-like inlets finally lead to Malin Head, the northernmost tip of Ireland.

One of the true wonders of nature is found at Giant's Causeway on the northern coast of County Antrim. Here 37,000 erect hexagonal basalt columns appear to have been perfectly and purposefully tiled together to form steps, pathways and staggered platforms extending down into the sea. The columns range in height from a few inches to the enormous pillars of the amphitheatre grouping, which reach heights of up to 80 feet. The scientific theory for the phenomenon goes back to a geological event of 60 million years ago when lava cooled as it surfaced, causing the crystallization of the rock. But far more interesting is the mythological explanation that tells of the great love of the giant Fionn MacCumhaill (Finn MacCool) for a giantess who lived on the island of Staffa along the Scottish coast. In order to reach his beloved, he threw stepping stones across the sea.

From heights of up to 2,000 feet, the Mourne Mountains sweep down to the sea in County Down. The Cooley Peninsula of County Louth provides wonderful views down the coast to Clogherhead.

South of Dublin in County Wicklow, known as the "garden of Ireland," Glendalough Forest Park encompasses a lake valley surrounded by the wooded Wicklow Mountains and is best known for its monastic ruins. Near Enniskerry, the Powerscourt Waterfall is the highest falls in Ireland, at nearly 400 feet. To the south, the Avondale Forest Park boasts a fine preserve of exotic trees. The coastal counties of Wexford and Waterford are low and flat, with long stretches of sandy beach and the driest climate on the island.

The southwestern coast of County Cork from Kinsale to Glengarriff offers varied and stunning seascapes, from fine sandy beaches to wild and rugged shores. Among the many small islands off the coast are Sherkin Island with its lovely beaches and prolific wildlife, and Cape Clear Island, which abounds in marine birdlife and provides a fantastic view of the Fastnet Rock Lighthouse (both islands are reached by boat from Baltimore). There is a discreet charm about the less touristy areas of Schull and Durrus, and the pastoral landscapes and small bays of the Sheep's Head Peninsula—the most

90 The coast of County Clare offers a variety of landscapes. Near Kilkee, a beautiful sandy beach gives rise to the dramatic cliffs of Castle Point, which stand 300 feet over the sea.

91-92-93-94 One of the most spectacular sights in Ireland, the Cliffs of Moher in northwest County Clare run for five miles along the coast and rise vertically from the pounding Atlantic at heights of up to 650 feet. The cliffs are home to a variety of seabirds, including puffins, and on a clear day provide a breathtaking view of the Aran Islands and the coasts of Galway to the north and Clare and Kerry to the south.

95 Green fields
surrounded by stone
walls suddenly give
rise to the rocky
plateau of the Burren
in County Clare. A
network of
underground caves
and "potholes" lie
beneath the unusual
landscape.

96 Typical images of
the Aran Islands off
the west coast of
Ireland. The three
islands, Inishmore,
Inishmaan and
Inisheer, have a
topography similar to
that of the Burren in
nearby County Clare,
and are barren reefs of
karstic limestone rock
where natives have
struggled to create tiny
patches of substitute
soil by layering seaweed
and sand. The maze of
high stone walls has
been created by the
clearing of rock from
the fields, and serves to
protect the small
"gardens" of crops from
the Atlantic gales. The
islanders have fished the
treacherous seas for
centuries in curraghs
or traditional canoes
covered with tarred
canvas, and ponies
and donkeys are still
the main means of
transport.

picturesque being Bantry Bay with its surrounding hills.

At Glengarriff, lush vegetation thrives in the warmth of the Gulf Stream mists, and fuschia, yews, and arbutus cover the slopes above the sea. The effect is amplified on nearby Garnish Island with its beautiful Italian gardens and splendid array of subtropical plants.

Within the heart of Ireland, the inland counties and regions offer endless stretches of bucolic scenery and peaceful waters. Many of Ireland's 800 loughs are scattered throughout the lakelands of Tipperary, Longford, Roscommon, Cavan, Leitrim and Monaghan—most of them formed by glacial action more than 10,000 years ago. Fishing is highly rewarding, and

boat rentals for vacation cruises are available throughout the district. The River Shannon, one of the longest rivers in Europe, rises in Cavan and runs south along the borders of Leitrim, Roscommon, Longford, Westmeath, Offaly, Galway, Tipperary, Clare and Limerick, where it meets the Atlantic. Its many loughs, tributaries and canals form a system of waterways that flow through lush midlands of verdant pastureland. The widest expanses of the Shannon are found at Lough Ree and Lough Derg, which are dotted with islands.

The enormity and diversity of Ireland's natural beauty cannot be chronicled within any singular body of text. There are new discoveries to be made in every corner of the island, from simple settings of soothing landscape to exhilarating vistas of startling terrain. Often a wrong turn or unexpected diversion will reveal the most pleasant surprises to those willing to add an element of adventure to their journey.

97 At the edge of the
limestone plateau on
the island of
Inishmore, Dun
Aenghus—one of the
most spectacular
prehistoric forts in
Europe—stands at
the edge of the cliff
which plunges 300
feet to the sea. Three
semicircular stone
walls outline the
ancient promontory
fort, with an outer
layer of sharp, erect,
stone slabs.
According to some
hypotheses, this was
originally a circular
fort, half of which fell
into the sea when a
section of the cliff
broke off.

*D*ublin is a city built on a small scale with an atmosphere of age, intimacy and slightly seedy elegance that delights natives and newcomers alike.

From its busy streets and grand public buildings to its narrow lanes of terraced houses, the city is bursting with character—a character that has been celebrated by its great writers, given a voice in its famous theatres, holds court in its old mahogany pubs and cafés, and is observed daily in her mundane yet eccentric traditions, from the quick-witted women of the Moore Street market to the horsedrawn carts that may still be seen transporting merchandise through the town.

But Dublin is also a vibrant, modern and culturally prolific city on the cutting edge of music, literature and film. It is a true European capital and centre for world commerce and industry. And it is a city teeming with the young, where babies' prams form an obstacle course around the city by day and hoards of teenagers dominate the streets by night.

The early Irish and official name of Ireland's capital, Baile Atha Cliath (Town of the Hurdle Ford), evolved in later times into Dubhlinn (Black Pool). Nearly one-third of the Republic's 3.5 million people live in and around Dublin, and like most of the world's cities, it is home to the nation's richest and poorest.

The city centre is divided into northside and southside by the River Liffey which flows east into Dublin Bay. The division is more than geographical and has traditionally aroused a subtle territoriality of social prejudices. While die-hard northsiders may regard the southside as posh and pretentious, some southsiders consider the neighborhoods north of the Liffey to be less than refined. But most Dubliners ignore the distinction, and are fiercely proud of their city as a whole, for it is that which sets them apart from the "culchies" of the countryside—a light-hearted rivalry in which the Irish revel. And in fact, most Dubliners today have "culchie" origins of which they are as proud as any native "Dub."

Though settled by the Vikings in the ninth century and fortified by the Anglo-Normans in the late Middle Ages, most of the large landmark structures that give Dublin its architectural personality were constructed during the veritable boom of building in the eighteenth century when the ruling British and the landed Anglo-Irish aristocracy built their neoclassical government structures, great mansions and townhouses, while simultaneously, poverty, squalor and misery blossomed in the deprived native slums of the city.

Beginning on the southside, the first area of the city centre to be explored runs south from O'Connell Bridge up to Stephen's Green, extends west to Christ Church and

98 top Parnell Sreet, Dublin. Located in the heart of the capital, the street is named in honour of Charles Stewart Parnell (1846–1891) the leader of the Irish Parliamentary Party and the Home Rule movement.

98-99 Across the Liffey over O'Connell Bridge is O'Connell Street, the widest commercial boulevard in Dublin. Originally called Sackville Street by the British, the name was changed in 1924 to commemorate "the Liberator", Daniel O'Connell (1775–1847), whose statue dominates the central island at the foot of the street. Among the other Irish leaders whose statues line the thoroughfare are the Home Rule champion Charles Stewart Parnell and the trade union leader Jim Larkin. In the middle of the avenue, the General Post Office (GPO), built in 1814, was the headquarters of the 1916 Easter Rising, which is commemorated by a statue and plaque inside the building.

99 top Running through the heart of Dublin is the River Liffey, which divides the city centre into the 'northside' and 'southside.' Here is shown a portion of the Ha'penny Bridge, an iron footbridge that owes its name to the toll (a halfpenny) that was originally charged to cross it in the early 19th century. The dome of the Custom House is visible beyond.

99 right The pedestrian thoroughfare of Grafton Street is the liveliest strip in the city, filled with busy shoppers, strollers, and "buskers". A traditional retreat from the bustling pace is found at Bewley's Cafés, a Dublin institution where the distinctive coffee and tempting pastries give solace to the weary, and where the atmosphere is ideal for a read or a chat. This area is the central shopping district of the city, and shops, cafés and restaurants catering to the downtown crowds are found in every direction off Grafton Street.

St. Patrick's Cathedrals, and east to Merrion Square. At the top of Westmoreland Street lies College Green, where the Bank of Ireland now occupies the imposing eighteenth-century building erected for the British-ruled Irish Parliament which assembled in Dublin only from 1782 until the Act of Union of 1801. Designed by the top architects of the day, Edward Lovett Pearce (Castletown House), James Gandon (Four Courts, Custom House) and

Francis Johnston (General Post Office), the former House of Lords may be viewed by request.

Across the way, the main entrance to Trinity College leads to a cobblestone quadrangle surrounded by the great halls of the university, most of which date from the eighteenth century. The college was established by Elizabeth I in 1592 to assure a loyalist, Protestant education to the ascendancy in an evil land of Popery. Though the obstacles to Catholic attendance were lifted by the end of the nineteenth century, the Catholic hierarchy's ban on their own flock's enrollment in the "godless institution" remained in effect until 1970.

Many well-known men of letters are counted among the alumni of Trinity College and include Jonathan Swift, Oliver Goldsmith, Oscar Wilde, J. M. Synge and Samuel Beckett, and several Irish Protestant nationalists such as Robert Emmet, Henry Grattan and Theobold Wolfe Tone. Here, the famous Book of Kells is on display in the Old Library, where a different page may be viewed each day.

College Green turns into Dame Street to the west, that leads past the Olympia Theatre and up Cork Hill to Dublin Castle, the headquarters of British rule in Ireland from the thirteenth century until 1922. The only remnant of the original Norman fortress is the Record Tower in the Lower Castle Yard. The grandly furnished State Apartments that once

101 top The Rock Garden, one of the liveliest spots in the revitalized Temple Bar district, attracts packed houses for performances by live bands.

were used for formal occasions may be toured, as well as the Bermingham Tower, where many Irish leaders as far back as Hugh O'Neill have been imprisoned. A sobering finale brings the visitor into the room where the wounded James Connolly, socialist leader of the 1916 Rising, was held before being brought to Kilmainham Jail for execution.

From here, Castle Street runs into Christ Church Place, where the first of Dublin's two cathedrals became Protestant at the time of the Reformation. The site of Christ Church Cathedral dates back to the original Viking church built here in 1038 by Sitric, the Norse King of Dublin. In 1173, the Anglo-Norman invader Strongbow built the stone structure, which received major reconstruction in the 1870s. The original crypt remains, as well as the north wall of the nave, the transepts and some sculptures. An effigy of a knight decorates what is reputed to be Strongbow's tomb in the south aisle.

In A.D. 841, the old Viking city of Dublin was established between Christ Church and Wood Quay on the Liffey. Excavations have uncovered sections of the original wall of the Hiberno-Norse city, as well as rows of tenth-century dwellings. Against stringent protests and public outcry, the excavation of this ancient city was halted by civic authorities in 1978 for the construction of a modern office block, an eyesore which not only destroyed the view of the Cathedral

overlooking the Liffey, but locked the buried treasures of the city's first settlement in cement.

A quarter of a mile away on Patrick Street is Dublin's second cathedral and Ireland's largest church, St. Patrick's. Founded in 1191 as a rival to Christ Church, the structure was completely renovated in the 1800s by the Guinness family. Jonathan Swift, who presided over the Cathedral for more than 30 years in the first half of the eighteenth century, is buried here. Swift dedicated his life to exposing the brutal indecency of English rule in Ireland.

Below Christ Church is the Brazen Head on Lower Bridge Street. The oldest pub in Dublin, it opened in 1688 and served as headquarters for the revolutionary United Irishmen at the end of the eighteenth century. Around the corner on Fishamble Street, nothing remains of the Musick Rooms where

104-105 Elizabeth I established Trinity College in 1592 as a Protestant university on the site of a confiscated monastery. Most of the buildings date from the 18th century, and surround a cobblestone quadrangle (top) that lies just beyond the main entrance at College Green. Illustrious alumni include Jonathan Swift, Oliver Goldsmith, Oscar Wilde, J. M. Synge, Samuel Beckett, and the revolutionary nationalists Robert Emmet and Theobold Wolf Tone. The spectacular Long Room of the Old Library houses over 200,000 of Trinity's three million volumes, including the Book of Kells, of which open pages of two sections are displayed daily.

105 top Across from the entrance to Trinity at College Green stands the 18th-century Bank of Ireland building, which served as the seat of the Irish Parliament for only 18 years, from 1782 until 1800, after which the Act of Union dissolved the body and Irish M.P.s sat at Westminster until 1922. The main part of the bank now occupies the former Court of Requests where petitions to the government were heard, and the original House of Lords may be toured by request.

Handel attended the first performance of his *Messiah* in 1742.

Back down Dame Street, Anglesea Street leads north into the Temple Bar area of narrow laneways that has recently seen an eclectic emergence of new cafés, shops, restaurants and art houses such as the Irish Film Centre. Back towards College Green, the city's main shopping district is dominated by the pedestrian thoroughfare of Grafton Street. The main branch of Bewley's Cafés is at No. 78/79, with the original stained glass windows by Harry Clarke. Along with the Westmoreland and South Great George's Street branches, Bewley's Oriental Cafés are a Dublin institution, and a time-honoured meeting place for coffee, conversation and a leisurely read of the newspaper. Besides the retailers on Grafton Street, the many side streets of the area contain interesting shops and malls including the Powerscourt Townhouse, Johnston's Court and the Westbury Mall.

At the top of Grafton Street lies Stephen's Green, a large square enclosing a pretty and tranquil park of gardens, lawns, duck ponds, a bandstand and assorted statuary of famous Dubliners. Surrounding the square are attractive Georgian houses, and on the north side, the striking Victorian-style Shelbourne Hotel, a Dublin landmark dating from 1865. Off the green on Dawson Street is the Mansion House, the Lord Mayor's official residence.

Down Kildare Street, Leinster House, built in 1745 from a design by Richard Cassels, has been the home of the Dáil Eireann (Irish Parliament) since 1922. Facing the parliament house, the National Library stands to the left and the National Museum to the right. The museum houses a fabulous collection of prehistoric artifacts, medieval ornamental objects and an exhibit devoted to the 1916 Rising and the War of Independence.

The National Gallery of Ireland on Merrion Square contains a collection of over 2,000 paintings including French Impressionists and Dutch masters, as well as many works by Jack B. Yeats and the Irish School. Merrion Square was the home of several famous Dubliners such as Oscar Wilde (No. 1), Daniel O'Connell (No. 58) and W. B. Yeats (Nos. 52 and 82).

Crossing the Liffey to the northside, the Ha'penny Bridge that graces the river to the west is named for the toll that was originally charged to cross it in 1816. At sunset on the Liffey, when the Dublin sky lights up in an extraordinary palette of colour, the delightful footbridge has a magical quality. On the north bank of the river, to the east stands the grand Custom House, and to the west, the elegant Four Courts building on Inns Quay. Both neoclassical structures were designed

105 bottom Overlooking O'Connell Street in the centre of Dublin is the statue of Daniel O'Connell, the Kerryman whose election forced the admission of Catholics to Parliament, where he secured the Catholic Emancipation Act of 1829.

106-107 The fanned transoms and brightly coloured doors of the elegant, 18th-century, Georgian residences are among Dublin's most attractive features. Examples of the architectural style, in vogue during the reign of George II (1727–1760) and George III (1760–1820), are best viewed around St. Stephen's Green, Merrion Square and Fitzwilliam Street and Square.

by James Gandon, built in the late eighteenth century and have been completely restored after fires reduced them to shells in the early 1920s during the Civil War.

Up the large boulevard of O'Connell Street are statues of some of the nation's leaders including Daniel O'Connell, Charles Stewart Parnell and James Larkin. The General Post Office, headquarters of the 1916 Rising, stands midway up the street. The pockmarks on the columns of the building's facade bear witness to the week-long battle. Inside, a bronze sculpture depicting the death of the Celtic mythological hero Cuchulainn commemorates the heroism of the rebels, as does a plaque inscribed with the Proclamation of the Irish Republic. At the top of O'Connell Street is Parnell Square, where the Rotunda Hospital, the Gate Theatre, the Municipal Gallery of Modern Art and the recently established Dublin Writers Museum are found. A few steps away, the Garden of Remembrance honours those who gave their lives for Irish freedom.

A quirky diversion on Dublin's northside is found at St. Michan's on Church Street. The dry atmosphere of the church's underground vaults has preserved a number of mummified bodies, and visitors are invited to "shake hands with a crusader or a nun" who lie receptively in open caskets.

The true Dublin experience also includes a visit to Ireland's National Theatre at the Abbey, a stroll in the vast Phoenix Park, an excursion by local DART train to the seaside villages of Dublin Bay including Howth and Dalkey. A visit to Kilmainham Jail, now a museum, was the incarceration site of generations of Irish patriots. It has held within its walls the United Irishmen and Eamon de Valera, who was released in 1924. The original facilities may be toured, including the yard where the 15 leaders of the 1916 Rising were shot by firing squad.

And then there are the pubs, where words flow as freely as Guinness, and where the art of "pulling a pint" is exceeded only by the intricacies of conversation. For fans of Joyce's *Ulysses*, requisite stops include Madigan's on North Earl Street, where the ornate decor includes a pendulum clock decreeing *tempus fugit*, and Davy Byrne's on Duke Street where Bloom stopped for his Gorgonzola cheese sandwich and glass of burgundy. Traditional Irish music is still a staple of O'Donoghues in Merrion Row, while Toner's and Doheny and Nesbitt's on Lower Baggot Street, and Mulligan's on Poolbeg Street have barely changed in 200 years. Great Victorian-style pubs include Ryan's of Parkgate Street and the Stag's Head in Dame Court. But among the many hundreds of Dublin pubs, individuals manage to find their favourite "local."

107 top The Victorian bandstand in Stephen's Green, the lovely park that occupies the square at the top of Grafton Street. Sir Arthur Guinness commissioned the landscaping of the common in 1877, which includes lawns, gardens, fountains, duck ponds, a playground, pavilion and statuary. Dubliners often follow the suggestion of the beloved ditty, The Dublin Saunter: "Dublin can be heaven, with coffee at eleven, and a stroll down Stephen's Green. No need to hurry, no need to worry..."

P hysical beauty, tumultuous history and rich cultural heritage are not unique to Ireland. Picturesque cottages and coastal cliffs exist elsewhere. Famine and oppression have defined many civilizations. And ancient ruins are found throughout the world.

Yet, this is a truly unique land.

Ireland's foremost distinction is her people, and the culture of the people that has survived in spite of the efforts of vations conquerors to obliterate it. The folk traditions of Western societies like Britain have always taken second place to an elite aesthetic of the upper classes. In Ireland, the reverse is true. Here, the aristocracy was foreign, thus their culture was eclipsed. And the popular ethos of Irish culture has manifested itself in many ways.

Its finest literature explores the domains of the working-class and the rural poor; its extraordinary music, song and dance has arisen from the humble kitchens, crossroads and pubs; and the heroes of its films are most often underdogs, outcasts and misfits. Its national heroes are champions of the oppressed who take on the mighty against the greatest of odds, usually losing the battle but winning the larger victory.

Ireland does have its symphony, galleries of fine art and ascendancy literature, its superstars, posh nightclubs and sophisticated society, but they are all still secondary and somewhat uncomfortably foreign. Through them the Irish maintain a common thread with the modern Western world. But it is within its deeply rooted native traditions that Ireland finds its identity. And perhaps the high esteem in which education, religion, language, folklore and the land are held is due to the long period when these basics of life were forbidden to the native Irish.

108 top A horseshoer at work. Horses are a vital part of Irish life, still commonly used throughout the country for carting and transport. The popular sports of horseracing, showjumping, hunting and riding also create a large demand for breeders.

108 centre Puck Fair, an annual festival held in Killorglin, County Kerry, is the scene of an important horse market every August. A young male goat or "puck" is crowned "king" at the start of the fair, and reigns over the festivities for three days.

108 bottom The annual Ould Lammas Fair in Ballycastle, County Antrim, is an enormous outdoor festival and market where everything, from dulse (a local delicacy of dried seaweed) to horses are on sale.

108-109 Horse-drawn carts are still seen throughout Ireland. Pictured here are the "jaunting cars" or pony-and-traps available for hire by tourists in the Killarney region of County Kerry.

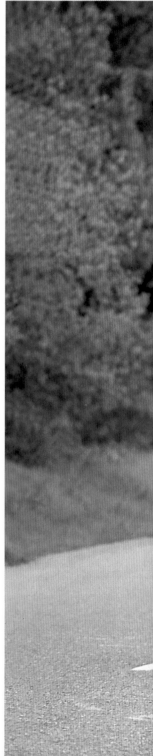

109 top left Colourful, handpainted, horse-drawn caravans may be rented for holiday vacations in several rural areas of Ireland, where visitors can enjoy a week reliving the old ways of the "travelling people," the gypsy lifestyle once common among the itinerant population of Ireland. Known as "tinkers"—a once derogatory name— the "travelers" still tend to live a life apart from the rest of the population, though most now reside in permanent, modern caravan (trailer) sites.

109 top right A young Irish girl. Ireland is a remarkably young country, where over half the population is under 25.

110 top More than a third of Connemara is bogland, consisting of a rich peat created by compacted layers of ancient vegetation which, due to a lack of oxygen in the waterlogged soil, never fully decomposed over thousands of years. Throughout rural Ireland, the peat is cut into small sods of turf that are stacked, dried and stored for use as a natural, pleasant-smelling fuel in stoves and hearths. Modern industrial harvesting of the bogs yields enough fuel for one-quarter of Ireland's electricity, as well as commercially produced peat briquettes for homes and peat moss for soil enrichment.

110-111 Sheep being transported in a marshy riverbed in County Sligo.

111 Sheepfarming is a major occupation in Ireland. Above, a sheep is sheared in an open field on the tiny island of Inishbofin, off the coast of Connemara. Below, a herd of sheep near the Burren in County Clare.

The quality of and respect for education in Ireland is renowned, some say a throwback to the Celtic reverence for learning and the scholarship of the early Irish monks. But the love of knowledge extends far beyond formal education, and in a society which defies stereotypes, aged farmers might expound on ancient Greece, while Dublin cabdrivers may be heard quoting *Ulysses*.

Catholicism is the dominant religion on the island, though it is not typically associated with a particularly strong religious fervor. Rather, it is an integral part of the indigenous society, an inherited practice with as many cultural incentives as spiritual. Pious demonstrations of faith are carried out in pilgrimages to the summit of Croagh Patrick, the shrine of Our Lady at Knock and the penitential island in Lough Derg. But when zealots perpetuated a phenomenon of moving, breathing and bleeding statues in the last decade, the anomalies attracted as many agnostic curiosity-seekers and fast-food vendors as the devout. And the irreverent humour of the ballads and commentaries that satirized these peculiarities has also cast its attention on the numerous clerical scandals that have shocked the faithful in recent years. Disillusionment presents a great challenge to all the churches in Ireland today, though they continue to maintain a stable foundation within society.

The love of sport that pervades all areas of the island is especially observed in the popular dedication to the native games of Gaelic football and hurling. Irish soccer fans boast a national team that has won universal admiration for its remarkable success in international competition, while sports such as tennis and rugby have smaller yet passionate followings. The Irish reputation for equestrian sports is longstanding, and Ireland's horses, breeders, trainers and jockeys are renowned throughout the world. Horseracing is a national obsession. Many spirited and festive equine events take place in Ireland each year, including the classy Irish Derby in the Curragh of Kildare, the festive Galway Races, the posh Dublin

112 and 113 top left
*Dingle Town, on the
Dingle Peninsula in
County Kerry, is an
active fishing port
and a popular tourist
destination in the
warmer months. A
strong Gaeltacht
(Irish-speaking) area,
many students come
here from all over the*

*country to enhance
their Irish language
skills in the summer.
The picturesque
village is dotted with
craft shops, art
galleries, seafood
restaurants, small
cafés and traditional
pubs, where Irish
music is often played.*

Horse Show and the traditional Ballinasloe Horse Fair.

The ancient Brehon Laws of the Irish Gaels contained strict codes of hospitality, requiring the members of the society to provide sustenance and comfort to visitors. An extraordinarily similar ethic of hospitality and generosity is seen in present-day Ireland, particularly in rural areas. And an inherent decency tends to pervade the society, where those in difficulty can often rely upon the support of neighbours. A visitor from London or New York will be struck by the sparsity of homeless people in the streets. An almost unanimous public consensus supports an infrastructure of social services that is remarkable in what was, until recently, a very poor country.

The Irish reputation for warmth, friendliness and conviviality tends to approach cliché, but the characterization is frequently confirmed. And it can be said that the Irish are a funny people. Though there are the serious, sour and pious individuals among them, the level of humour in the country is perhaps unparalleled.

Often the wit is founded in irreverence, and the Irish are constantly reminding Ireland not to take itself too seriously. An example is

113 bottom left *The
Victorian
harbourfront of
Newcastle, County
Down, sits at the foot
of the Mourne
Mountains on the
Irish Sea's Dundrum
Bay.*

113 right *Fishing is a
major industry in
Ireland, as well as a
significant tourist
attraction. Deep-sea
and fresh-water fish
abound and the
country is renowned
for its salmon and
trout. Seafood dishes*

*are an Irish speciality,
and people travel from
around the world to
sample Galway oysters,
which are best enjoyed
at cottage restaurants
such as Moran's of the
Weir (below right) off
the main road in
Clarinbridge.*

114-115 Catholic pilgrims climb to the summit of Croagh Patrick, Ireland's sacred mountain, where St. Patrick is believed to have fasted for forty days and forty nights, and from where he is said to have banished the snakes from Ireland. The intensely devout make the trek barefoot over a steep terrain of rough rocks. The holy journey may be carried out at any time of the year, but the traditional date for the pilgrimage is the last Sunday in July, when tens of thousands begin the climb at dawn, and assemble at the top for Mass.

found in the recent efforts to dress up Dublin with sculptures of two of its beloved fictional characters. The sensuous Anna Livia was Joyce's personification of the River Liffey—an earthy likeness of the lady lounging in a pool of water became dubbed overnight as "the floozie in the Jacuzzi;" the same fate befell poor Molly Malone, the unfortunate fishmonger whose wheelbarrowed effigy was immediately christened "the tart with the cart."

But when the irreverence turns spiteful, the activity is known to the Irish as "begrudgery." Because of it, success can become an uncomfortable experience here, a phenomenon which is, however, not unknown in many other countries of the world.

As with any group who share a repressed background, the Irish enjoy a remarkable bond. Their common points of reference can bring the quality of a perpetual school reunion to their discourse. And that camaraderie involves an historical inclination to mistrust authority and maintain a vague, unspoken pact against it. Rules and regulations are often skirted with "a wink and a nod," a practice which at times appears to enjoy the mandate of the entire country.

The pub has its own unique character in this society. As an institution in Irish life, its role is something of a communal living room, a focal point of social contact.

Even in large towns and cities, the Irish traditionally do not socialize at home. That function is conveniently fulfilled by the public house. Whether one arrives from a palatial mansion, a one-room flat or a crumbling cottage, a common ground is found at the "local" where young and old, rich and poor may mingle with ease. Indeed, the Irish navigate their cities as much by reference to the landmarks of popular pubs as by such mundane means as street names.

And in Ireland, the country and the people are inextricably connected. Here, there is a story to every acre of land, every mound of earth, every cottage and every laneway. Every house and every street in every corner of every town is imbued with tales. The stories personify the place. The physical Ireland is happenstance; the island is an entity of human past and human presence. Places assume character, environs are companions. The ditch, the field and the doorway are comforting friends, so that the pitch dark night loses its menace and the long road is less lonely. The Irish people have been repeatedly robbed of their physical land, but only temporarily; a body and its soul cannot be divided.

118-119
Horseracing is pursued with a vigour in Ireland, where meetings range from the elegant Irish Derby, held each June in the Curragh of Kildare, to the eccentric Laytown Strand Races which are run annually in August on the beach at Laytown, County Meath, and are scheduled to coincide with low tide. At least 300 days of horseracing are run each year on the country's two dozen racetracks. Some go on for days, such as those in Galway, Tralee and Listowel. The Curragh of Kildare is horse country, 6,000 acres of grassy plain that are home to some of the best stables and finest thoroughbreds in the world. Next to the racetrack is the

Irish National Stud and the Irish Horse Museum. Besides the Irish Derby, several other prestigious races are held here, including the One Thousand Guineas, run in May, where fast and furious betting, ebullient enthusiasm and elegant attire are the order of the day.

120 top and 121 The granite exterior of Cobh's St. Colman's Cathedral is adorned with statues, and its tall, spired bell tower houses the largest carillon in Ireland, with over over 40 bells.

The Irish have always maintained a fierce territorial competitiveness; allegiances to home villages, towns and counties extend far beyond the loyalties associated with sports. But in the cities, pride of origin and place is so powerfully innate as to appear genetic.

Cork's rivalry with Dublin is legendary, and is only exceeded by its fondness for itself. But the natives are right, there is a great deal to admire about Cork, a beautiful port city whose central district forms an island between the two branches of the

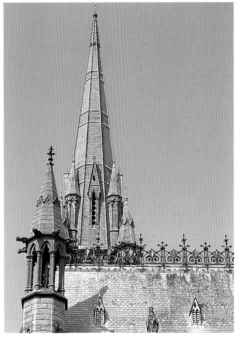

River Lee. The city is surrounded by a series of beautiful quays and bridges, crowned by numerous church spires and distinguished by its eighteenth-century, bow-windowed Georgian houses.

Cork, the third largest city in Ireland after Dublin and Belfast, is the capital of the south. Corcaigh—Irish for "marshy land"—was established in the seventh century around the ancient monastery of St. Finbarr. The

merchant city has always maintained a prosperous harbour of shipping and shipbuilding, as well as successful industries including distilling and brewing—Murphy's Stout and Beamish Stout are made here. The old Cork Butter Exchange fell into disuse in 1924, but the neoclassical structure served as the hub of the one of the world's largest butter trades for 150 years, which was largely responsible for the city's economic and physical

120-121 Cork's River Lee runs out to Cork Harbour, where the town of Cobh (pronounced "cove"), once known as Queenstown, was the main point of embarkation for emigrants to North America, as well as passengers on transatlantic oceanliners. The town is dominated by the splendid, neo-Gothic St. Colman's Cathedral, a 19th-century Roman Catholic church set on the hill overlooking the harbour. Today, the picturesque harbour of Cobh is a tourist destination and a yachting centre. The Queenstown/Cobh Heritage Centre contains exhibits on the Irish emigrant experience (including genealogical records and passenger lists) and the great transatlantic ships, including the Titanic, whose last port-of-call was Cobh, and the Lusitania which was sunk off these shores by a German submarine in 1915. Rescue boats from Cobh retrieved some of the bodies which were buried in the Old Church Cemetery, and a memorial to the 1,198 victims stands in Roger Casement Square.

growth. It now houses the artisans' shops of the Shandon Craft Centre.

The steep slope of Patrick's Hill rises to the north, where the landmark Shandon Steeple of St. Anne's Church and the tower of St. Mary's dominate the skyline. The Shandon Bells are so sonorous that they became immortalized in a popular song. Resembling a peppermill, the bell tower is curiously multicoloured, built of red sandstone on two sides, and grey limestone on the others.

The city's main crossing is St. Patrick's Bridge which leads into the main thoroughfare of St. Patrick's Street, or Pana as its known to the locals. The lively street winds into the heart of the city and the main shopping district. To find Cork's oldest neighborhood, one must cross to the south bank, where the old city grew up around Finbarr's ancient monastery. The site is occupied today by St. Finbarr's Cathedral, a spectacular nineteenth-century French Gothic-style structure with fabulous painted ceilings and mosaics. Nearby, the Red Abbey Tower, which happens to be grey, is the only remains of an Augustinian priory of the 1300s.

The famine devastated this area of the country, and most of the "coffin ships" which carried survivors to North America left from Cobh in Cork Harbour. "Rebel Cork" has earned its nickname well; it was the headquarters of the revolutionary Fenian Movement of the nineteenth century and saw some of the most intense fighting of the Civil War in the 1920s, when much of the city burned to the ground.

Cork is known for its liberal intellectualism and is home to one of the National University of Ireland's three colleges, University College, Cork or UCC. The Cork Film Festival is internationally renowned, and its jazz festival is a major national event. The people of Cork have their own distinct brand of humour, delivered in rapid and melodious speech that often baffles non-natives.

Limerick is next in size to Cork and was originally established as a Viking stronghold on the banks of the River Shannon. After Brian Boru

122-123 The main thoroughfare of Patrick Street in downtown Cork City runs through the middle of a busy commercial area and bustling shopping district. Surrounded by the two main branches of the River Lee, a maze of quays and bridges join the town centre to the rest of Cork, adding a lovely atmosphere to the port city. Narrow lanes and eclectic architecture add a special charm, as does the city's seat of higher learning, University College, Cork (UCC).

124 top The Union Theological College of the Presbyterian Church on Botanic Avenue in Belfast. Neoclassical style dominates much of the city's urban architecture.

124-125 In front of Belfast's imposing City Hall building lies Donegall Square, a green containing a statue of Queen Victoria and a memorial to the victims of the Titanic which was built in a Belfast shipyard.

125 top Sir Charles Lanyon designed the Tudor-style, red-brick buildings of Belfast's Queens University in the mid-19th century, following models from Oxford University. Then known as Queens College, it received university status in 1908.

125 centre The exquisite Palm House at Belfast's Botanic Gardens consists of a cast-iron frame fitted with curved glass panels. The Victorian landmark was begun in 1839, and is one of the oldest structures of its kind in the world.

125 bottom Dominating the centre of Belfast is the enormous, neoclassical City Hall building, completed in 1906. Each of the four corners are topped by towers and the structure is crowned with a 173-foot-high copper dome.

defeated the Danes, the Anglo-Normans took over in the thirteenth century and built thick walls around their fortress to exclude the natives, hence dividing the town into what is still known as the old district of "English Town" to the north, and "Irish Town" to the south. The fortress of King John's Castle built in 1210 is one of the oldest Norman structures in Ireland. Three of the four original round-towered corners survive on the five-sided courtyard castle. Part of the medieval town wall can be seen off Old Clare Street, .

In the west of Ireland, the small city of Galway is known for its strong tradition of arts and culture, and its lively, cosmopolitan air. Like Cork, Galway is a university town and is enlivened by its young student population. The city forms a network of narrow streets, islands, bridges and quays that merges on the banks of the River Corrib and its tributaries as it flows towards Galway Bay.

The original ancient settlement here was fortified in the thirteenth century by the Normans who built a wall around the city to keep out the "wild Irish." Because of the fourteen wealthy merchant families who dominated in the sixteenth and seventeenth centuries, Galway became known as the City of the Tribes. Lynch's Castle on William Street is an example of one of their tower houses. The Spanish influence in the carved detail of the doorway reflects the strong trading links between Galway and Spain which developed as early as the fifteenth century. A section of the city wall can be seen extending from Spanish Arch in the dock area.

The centre of town runs from Eyre Square, down William and Shop Streets and across High Street to Quay Street. St. Nicholas' Collegiate Church on Market Street was founded by the Anglo-Normans in 1320. Though extensively restored in later years, it retains much of its medieval character, and the marks of Cromwell's destructive siege are still visible within.

The city's cultural offerings, including two established theatre companies and a wealth of live traditional music in the pubs, are bolstered by the Galway Arts Festival in July. Galway Race Week is held in the same month and is a festive and

jovial gathering for horseracing fans and "holiday-makers." This is oyster country, where the Galway Oyster Festival in September celebrates the first harvest of the season.

Though known throughout the world for its role in the Northern Ireland conflict, Belfast is a large, industrial, working-class city as well as the commercial and cultural capital of the province. Here, rusty barbed wire, abandoned check-points and nationalist political murals along the Shankill Road coexist with the elegant downtown of Victorian Belfast. The once thriving linen and shipbuilding industries that made it an important and wealthy port and trading centre have since declined, but the drydock of the Harland and Wolff yard is still the largest in the world, and ship repair and construction continue to be a significant occupation. Circled by hills, the city is built around the River Lagan which flows into Belfast Lough and the North Channel sea.

The city centre is reserved for pedestrians and the bustling shopping district stretches from the neoclassical, copper-domed City Hall in Donegall Square, north to St. Anne's Cathedral. In the square, a statue of Queen Victoria is a reminder of the monarch's great influence on Belfast, to which she granted a city charter in 1888. The gardens also contain a monument commemorating the *Titanic,* which was built in the city's shipyards, and the Linen Hall Library dating from the late 1700s. Donegall Place meets Castle Place which leads through High Street to the leaning Albert Memorial Clock Tower and the River Lagan. Here, two gigantic cranes known as "Samson and Goliath" tower above the city's shipyards.

To the south, Great Victoria Street is known as the Golden Mile, and is a restaurant and nightlife district home to the ornate, Victorian-style Grand Opera House. Opposite the Europa Hotel, the Crown Liquor Saloon is a national monument which still functions as a

127 top Muckross House, on the shores of Muckross Lough in Killarney National Park, County Kerry, one of the most popular tourist destinations in Ireland. The 19th-century, Tudor-style manor house is surrounded by a splendid garden of rhododendrons and azaleas. It is home to the Kerry Folklife Centre, a museum and research centre for natural history and native crafts.

pub. Its carved oak "snugs," shiny brass fittings, old gas lamps and coloured tiles provide a delightful atmosphere. The narrow lanes off High Street are filled with interesting shops and lovely Victorian pubs. White's Tavern—the oldest pub in the city dating from 1630—is a cosy hostelry with an open fire.

Another city of Georgian doorways and grand public buildings, Derry stands on the River Foyle, which flows into the Atlantic bay of Lough Foyle. The city's most notable feature is its walls, which are 25 feet high and reach 30 feet in thickness. A terrace walkway atop the stone ramparts, which extend for a mile around the centre, provide a good perspective of the old city. From the Diamond which serves as the central square, four main streets radiate to the Shipquay, Ferryquay, Bishop's and Butcher's Gates of the enclosure.

Union Hall Street near Shipquay Gate leads to the O'Doherty's Tower which houses the Tower Museum and the "Story of Derry" exhibition, a comprehensive historical introduction to the city. Butcher's Gate leads to the nationalist Catholic Bogside district, where Free Derry Corner is dominated by the enormous mural covering a gabled wall which announces "You are now entering Free Derry."

St. Columba founded a monastery at Derry (Doire, "oak grove") in the sixth century. Down the street from the impressive arch of Bishop's Gate, the Gothic-style St. Columba's Cathedral was built in 1633 and was a significant defensive position in the 1688-1689 Siege of Derry by the deposed Catholic king of England, James II. Though thousands starved to death as a result of the blockade, the Protestant resistance to the 105-day siege gave birth to the loyalist slogan of "No Surrender" which endures in Northern Ireland to this day.

Beyond the city walls stands the Guildhall, a red sandstone neo-Gothic structure built in 1890. Its richly decorated exterior includes a fabulous four-faced clock spire and stained-glass windows that depict the significant events of Derry's history.

128-129
Portstewart, a quiet
resort on the northern
coast of County
Derry, is known
primarily for its three
mile beach,
Portstewart Strand,
a wide expanse of
golden sand on the
Atlantic coast near
the mouth of the
River Bann.

129 top Old houses
along the quays in
Galway City overlook
the harbour of
Galway Bay on the
west coast of Ireland.

129

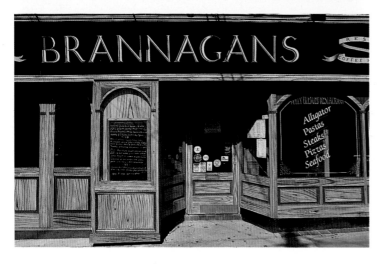

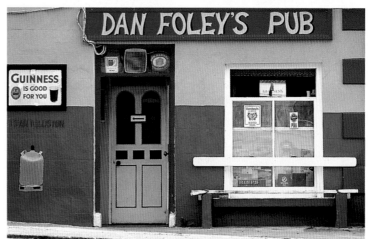

130 Throughout Ireland, ancient doorways and old buildings are handpainted in brilliant colours and decorated with rich woodwork to create beautiful traditional shopfronts and striking pub and restaurant facades.

131 Whimsical fancy often inspires improvisational signpainters who leave their mark on the outside of Irish pubs, while the work of true artisans may be admired in the more intricate and sophisticated detail of traditional handpainted signs.

136 The colourful facade of a Galway shop specializing in woollens and handknits, a traditional Irish industry.

INDEX

MUSEUM AND ART COLLECTIONS

ILLUSTRATION CREDITS

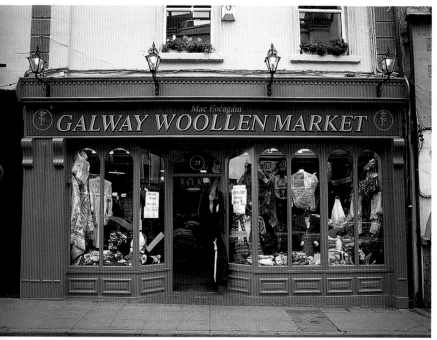